M000073908

CHILDREN:
Blessing
or
Burden?

CHILDREN:
Blessing
or
Burden?

Exploding the Myth of the Small Family

MAX HEINE

NOBLE PUBLISHING ASSOCIATES
GRESHAM, OREGON

NOBLE PUBLISHING ASSOCIATES, the publishing arm of Christian Life Workshops, is an association of Christian authors dedicated to serving God and assisting one another in the production, promotion, and distribution of audio, video, and print publications. For instructions on how you may participate in our association or for information about our complete line of materials write to:

NOBLE PUBLISHING ASSOCIATES
P.O. Box 2250
Gresham, Oregon 97030

or call (503) 667-3942.

Copyright © 1989 by Max Heine

All rights reserved. No part of this book may be reproduced in any form without permission in writing from the publisher, except in the case of brief quotations embodied in critical articles or reviews.

All Scripture references are taken from The New American Standard Bible, copyright © by The Lockman Foundation, 1960, 1962, 1963, 1968, 1971, 1973, 1975, 1977. Used by permission.

ISBN: 0-923463-94-1
Printed in the United States of America.

To Edie,
a fruitful wife,
whose children rise up and bless her

ACKNOWLEDGEMENTS

I thank the authors who have diligently researched and published before me on most of the themes in this book, particularly Jacqueline Kasun, Julian Simon, George Gilder, Ben Wattenberg, Gary North and Mary Pride. Most helpful of all have been the penetrating newsletters of Allan Carlson and Bryce Christensen at the Rockford Institute Center for the Family in America. Their consistently insightful pronatalist essays, along with their current synopses of family-related academic journals, have long since scooped me on several issues in this book. They are indispensable for anyone who wants a keen understanding of the complex family/state issues facing today's world. to subscribe, write to *The Family in America*, P.O. Box 416, Mount Morris, IL 61054.

In ways less tangible but no less significant, I am indebted to Michael Ford and other men and women at Christian Family Church. We have quietly tried in teaching and in practice to scrape away the modern muck that has obscured the foundation stones related to family. This is not to say that we are heirs to God's perfect revelation of family, or that this book is an official policy statement, for it is not. I can say only that I am blessed, not just with children, but with faithful friends willing to work out their salvation and that of their families' with fear and trembling. Had I not been in that climate, this book would not have come to be.

ACKNOWLEDGMENTS

CONTENTS

PART I: THE PROBLEM

Introduction 13

1 / The Flight From Procreation 23
2 / Abandoned Preschoolers, Dormant Teens 39

PART II: THE FOUNDATION

3 / Be Fruitful and Multiply 55
4 / The Hebrew Family 67

PART III: THE CHOICE

5 / Birth Control: Right or Wrong? 87
6 / Building a Better Incubator 109

PART IV: THE PRIVATE PICTURE

7 /   Motherhood: The Neglected Career..............125
8 /   Parenthood's Deep Currents of Blessing 149

PART V: THE BIG PICTURE

9 /   Growing Populations 169
       Their Benefits, Their Enemies
10 / China's Self-inflicted Genocide....................193
11 / Sweden: America's Forerunner?...................205

PART VI: CONCLUSION

12 / Prosperity and Posterity 225

Endnotes...239

PREFACE

This is not another book about how to be a Supermom or Superdad. There are lots of those books around. I encourage you to read them. If you're like me, you need all the help you can get.

What this book does offer is a challenging look at the role of procreation in the family and society. There is more to the Master's design for family and to His plan for families to proliferate throughout the earth, than meets the eye.

INTRODUCTION

H ey, Dad, you've got to come see my target practice," says son Isaac, pausing from hurling red clay mud balls at a crayoned circle on the newly painted house. "Look, I got one right in..."

"I know—I'll just chain him to his bed whenever he's not in school," thinks Abe, after barking orders to hose down the wall. "I'll cut a hole in the bottom of his door, yeah, and we can slip his meals through."

Abe, thirty-four, has just finished another long Friday at the bank, where he processes loans. He senses—from the mud mural, the strewn garden tools, the competing screams of his wife and youngest child that are audible even before he opens the back door—that the day still has a long way to go. If only someone had given him a loan. Enough energy and patience to make it through the night—that's all he would need to borrow.

"Well, how nice of you to drop in, Abe," snaps Sarah. Her voice strains to be heard above the screams of one-year-old Jacob, who forms a perfect crescent as he arches his back on the kitchen floor. "Your son flushed his dirty diaper down the commode while I was on the phone with your mother, who was telling me that Isaac doesn't pronounce his 'th' properly, and he'll probably need speech therapy—that is, assuming he's not retarded—and by the way, you know, we never replaced that window pane he broke in their den, and she says the wind's coming in and making your father's arthritis act—"

"Hold on," interrupts Abe. He picks up writhing Jacob, whose thrashing head smears well-chewed fruit cocktail on Daddy's favorite tie. Abe collapses in a chair. He suddenly realizes he's made a direct hit on the congealed ice cream and chocolate syrup from last night's dessert fest. He summons his mental reserves, depleted from a day of punching buttons on calculators and telephones and a night of padding the floor with a sleepless Jacob, to focus on the biggest brush fire: "Did the toilet back up from the diaper?"

"Just make sure you've got your galoshes on when you go upstairs," says Sarah.

"Okay," grunts Abe. He tries to shift in his sticky seat, indulging in a few seconds of strange quiet that envelops the kitchen. He calculates the number of hours until all the kids are in bed, the dust begins to settle, and he can relax on his recliner with that new spy novel. Maybe catch something on the tube. Suddenly a cold spray of water through the open window—darling Isaac has inserted comic relief into his window washing—jolts Abe back to terra firma. Jacob resumes crying.

"Oh," says Sarah. "The dentist said there's no big problem with Rachel's teeth."

Thank goodness. "A point for the home team," thinks Abe.

"He said a good orthodontist should have her straightened out in five or six years. Said it should only be $2,500."

Only?

This modern-day Abe is having a little trouble living up to his Biblical namesake, who was called "exalted father" (Abram) and "father of a multitude" (Abraham). Many of us can sympathize with the musings of this twentieth-century Abraham and Sarah: "If these little creatures are blessings, Lord, keep the curses far, far away."

This book aims to magnify God's simple declaration that children are a literal blessing. It will help Christian parents get their ideas about kids in line with God's perspective—not to enthrone children, as some are prone to do, but to show that children should be a natural product of marriage. It will explain how today's parents are challenged to establish a godly family order in which it becomes much easier to acknowledge that children really are God's unqualified blessing. It will expose the secular myth that the world is over-populated and the resulting global campaigns to abort babies, kill infants, and sterilize adults. It will show that the Bible is by no means silent about God's desire for families to be prolific as part of completing His Genesis mandate to fill the earth.

At the same time, there'll be no pious double-talk that sugarcoats with Scripture the grisly reality of raising children. A commitment to raise a family takes up a big chunk of adulthood. As we will see, unless parents are following godly principles along the way, their children may well become curses to them instead of blessings.

Face it: Children are expensive. They rob you of sleep. They get in the way. They get dirty. They demand everything. They're ungrateful. They break things. They mess up your household projects. They cut into your time. They dash dreams of carefree vacations. They tie up your phone. They commandeer your car. They grow up and give you worries.

It's no exaggeration to say they require everything from A to Z. They need to be Answered, Bathed, Combed, Diapered, Encouraged, Fed, Groomed, Helped, Instructed, Judged, Kissed, Led, Managed, Nurtured, Observed, Praised, Quieted, Reminded, Spanked, Trained, Utilized, Valued, Wedded, X-rayed, and Yearned for Zealously. And before, during, and after all of that, they need to be loved—which is sometimes hardest of all.

In other words, it's easy to reckon children strictly as liabilities. Our contemporary Sarah does. Her day has been a blur of child-related tasks that seem, she hates to admit, pointless and endless. Fixing school lunches, driving car pool, stopping twice at the day-care center so she can work part time at a friend's new gift store, changing diapers, washing clothes, washing the kitchen floor, washing dishes, washing dried food off the wall, washing, washing, washing....Then Abe has the nerve to come home and wonder why she doesn't find time to wash the windows and replace the buttons on his ratty old shirts. She would have time and energy for that, and for planting a garden, and maybe playing tennis as they used to, and, who knows, even some late-night cuddling on the couch, if only, if only....

If only it weren't for children. That's what Sarah thinks, though not out loud.

Many people today, however, are not just thinking about the "problem" of children. They're employing defensive tactics. That's why family size is decreasing. That's why couples postpone having children—or the child—until they're "ready." That's why birth control is such an accepted part of the culture of industrialized nations and why abortion and infanticide are rapidly attaining equal tolerance, contributing to the suicidal depopulation trends of many nations. That's why people—including Christians—have allowed the state to usurp normal functions of family nurturing, resulting in growing alienation between generations, from cradle to grave.

Christian parents in this climate have little incentive to depart from the prevailing world view. Many simply don't know any better. Yet the Bible challenges parents to adopt a different perspective. Psalm 127:3-5 offers the most succinct statement of how God values children and large families:

> Behold, children are a gift of the Lord;
> The fruit of the womb is a reward.
> Like arrows in the hand of a warrior,
> So are the children of one's youth.
> How blessed is the man whose quiver is full
>   of them;
> They shall not be ashamed,
> When they speak with their enemies in the
> gate.

How do Christian parents resolve this conflict between what the Word of God says and what their eyes (and wallets) are telling them? When should young couples start having children? How do parents of two or four or eight children decide to expand their family further? What about overpopulation? Is birth control OK? Should a mother stay home with young children? How can children be financial blessings? Can parents really be blessed by children, or is this just a Biblical euphemism?

Many Christian parents answer these questions no differently from non-Christians. Little do they realize that what they consider normal attitudes and values regarding children are actually radical departures from Biblical—and sometimes time-tested secular—family norms. Today's norm regarding procreation and motherhood is a status quo prophesied by radicals, forged by cultural trends, and perpetuated by desperate, often distant, parents willing to look for answers anywhere but in the Bible.

Where deception has come to reign, Christian parents need to shine the light of God's eternal truth. There are Biblical principles regarding procreation and family that do not evolve with secular trends and denominational accommodations. Christian parents must be like those in the Bible who "understood the times" (1 Chr. 12:32).

Today's Christian family, in fact, has the unusual opportunity to be a beacon to a selfish and literally perishing generation merely by the way it values children. The world says children are an intrusion. The redeemed family puts out the welcome mat. The world looks to day care, schools, peer groups, and any other surrogate parent institution to shoulder the burden of children's training. The redeemed family takes primary responsibility for raising children and presents them to the world as God's promised blessings come true.

This is where the "rubber meets the road" in parents' efforts to resist the burden mentality and walk in the reward-blessing perspective described in Psalm 127. Parents must replace the attitude of liability with one of godly investment. The money, time, sleeplessness, inconvenience, worry, and heartache required to bring a child from conception to adulthood—these things cost, and they hurt. But not one dime, not one midnight walk of the floor with a sick one, is wasted.

The Bible says repeatedly we will reap what we sow. The Christian parent is not sowing ultimately toward construction of a student, grass-cutter, or highly paid computer programmer—though parents should aspire to train productive children who will eventually contribute much more than they consume, one of many practical aspects of the child-blessing. Rather, mothers and fathers are building men and women who will impact society, just like those at the city gates described in Psalm 127:5—spiritual warriors willing to stand in the public arena, without shame, and confront God's enemies.

The Bible says a man is blessed to have a quiver full of children. May each parent be prepared to receive that reward and to be faithful over it so that it yields God's intended return—for the sake of the child and the family, for the church and society.

PART 1

THE PROBLEM

ONE

THE FLIGHT
FROM PROCREATION

... for they have demoralized the builders.
(Nehemiah 4:5)

P regnant women bothered Maurice Utrillo. When the French painter saw them on the street, "he would chase them and pull their hair and try to kick them in the stomach."[1]

Utrillo was a little less inhibited than many modern Americans in expressing a low regard for maternity. He was no less violent, though. Nowadays even expectant mothers can't be trusted. Every year, 1,600,000 women in America seek out the abortionist, submitting to the internal violence of the vacuum hose or bone-crushing forceps.

What has been less publicized than the abortion struggle is that women in America and other industrialized nations are having fewer and fewer babies. Couples are failing to reproduce at rates that will replace the current population. We are surrounded by people, many of them with high intelligence and earning power, who calmly refuse to bear children.

For example, Karen Rohde, forty—an obstetrician, no less—was childless and devoted to her second marriage and her career. She had some regrets about missing the receiving end of obstetrical care, but she has adjusted. "Time got away from me....Whenever I see a particularly sweet-looking baby, I just think of what they're like when you take them home. Then I'm glad I'm not the one who has to lose sleep taking care of them."[2]

God's gift of children has always been a mixture of burden and blessing, of losing sleep and finding deep satisfaction. The Bible unequivocally says they are a blessing; in our fallen world, we experience children in varying degrees as burdens, as they impinge on typically self-centered lives. The rise in child abuse is evidence enough that children are clearly unwelcome for many adults.

The trend toward having fewer children has virtually convinced some people that it is impossible to have a large family these days. Or at least it is impossible to have one *and* be happy and sane.

Not so. For example, Roy and Elizabeth Heyne of South Lake, Texas, had eight children under thirteen years old, along with a pony, cows and chickens in their fenced-in yard. Six children per family was the norm among their closest friends. One family had thirteen.

"Our get-togethers would boggle the minds of most people," Roy said. "When we entertain at home, which we do fairly often, it's not unusual to have groups of forty."

Mrs. Heyne frankly admits that being a working mother—a certified physician's assistant—is harder than completing graduate school.

"Every night I fall into bed exhausted, but every morning I wake up excited, looking forward to the day. No matter how draining it is or how much organization and effort it takes, I feel certain that this is the happiest time of my life."[3]

The Heynes' willingness to have a quiver full of children and devote their free time to family activities would have been unremarkable in earlier times. Today, this kind of family stands out. That's because the general perception of children has shifted much farther toward the burden side of the family and social ledgers. There are many varied and complex reasons for this change of heart. Some of them are valid reasons, such as the shift toward extended education that happens as an agricultural society becomes an industrialized one.

On the other hand, some reasons are selfish and directly contrary to Scripture. Consequently, Western society is beginning to reap the fruits of rejecting what God has deemed a blessing. This book will explore the dark corners of this modern obsession to shun procreation and the resulting chaos that has begun to emerge. The good news is that there is a redemptive trail upon which the church can lead. It is not so much a new trail to be blazed as it is an old one that is overgrown.

Baby Bust

American Quaker families in the eighteenth century were no strangers to childbearing. Having babies and raising children was a forty year endeavor. When the last birdie flew the coop, Mother was about sixty years old.

So just how many babies were there? Around 1790, American women were having about seven. Only a hundred years later, that rate had dropped to four per woman. Today, that rate is slightly below the rate of 2.1 needed to sustain the population.

Demographer Ben Wattenberg called this "the birth dearth" in his important 1987 book of the same title. This major decline in births is doubly shocking in that it has come so suddenly after the baby boom. It seems somebody gave a sudden push to the fertility pendulum.

The baby boom peaked in 1957, when the total fertility rate (the rate of births for women projected over their fertile years) reached 3.77. Then it plunged by more than half to 1.74 in 1976. It has held at about 1.8 through most of the 1980s.[4] By 1989, it had climbed to 1.97.

America has not suffered from the baby bust as much as some European nations because we are still feeling the impact of the baby boom. There are now a large number of baby boom mothers in their fertile years. They are not having large families, but there are so many of them that they're producing an apparently adequate baby population.

The crunch comes in about forty years. Unless attitudes on procreation change, the small-to-moderately sized cohort of baby boomers' children will be having even fewer children. That means fewer potential mothers with each generation. American society will be populated more and more by older citizens. Even if childbearing habits change, it will take generations to reverse the momentum and restore the demographic equilibrium.

The results of a dwindling population are economically and politically catastrophic. To avoid collapse, Social Security will demand increased taxes and reduced benefits as the worker-retiree ratio drops. The balance is further skewed because baby boomers and subsequent generations probably will live even longer than our parents, thanks to improving health care.

The centuries-old growth constant that has fueled the dynamo of capitalism will be gone. Virtually every market will suffer—housing, automobiles, education, you name it. When consumers are scarce, capitalism flounders. Children are a blessing to the free market because they are the growth upon which it depends.

What also bothers Wattenberg is the shift in cultural and political weight. America appears destined to have a population with a higher proportion of non-European immigrants (who are not afraid to procreate) and the elderly. It's debatable as to whether the immigrant issue poses a major problem, or whether it is "racist" (as Wattenberg was accused of being) to worry about it.

There is clearly trouble, though, when a society's median age climbs too much. After all, the young are the workers, the producers, the innovators. A swelling rank of senior citizens means preoccupation with meeting basic needs—health care, retirement income, housing and the like. In some countries today, as in America's past, these were needs shouldered by family members, especially children, of the elderly. But now, more people will be entering retirement with fewer children. And with young adults willing to relocate in pursuit of careers, even those elderly with children will be lucky to have any living close enough to be of any help.

Shrinking Christendom

The full impact of the impending cultural shift Wattenberg predicted involves more than just the elderly. To understand, we need to look at the global picture.

Many countries are more adamant than America in seeing children as burdens. Using figures from 1985 (or the latest available), Wattenberg found that West Germany had the distinction of having the lowest total fertility rate in the world—1.3. Trailing close behind at 1.4 were Italy, Luxembourg and Denmark. Other modern, industrialized, free nations with rates below the replacement level of 2.1 were Canada, Sweden, Japan, Belgium, Austria, Switzerland, Finland, France, United Kingdom, Norway, the Netherlands, Iceland, Spain and Australia.

So what's the rest of the world doing? The former Communist-bloc countries were growing steadily with a total fertility rate of 2.3. Third World peoples are mushrooming at 4.1—serious procreating, but considerably lower than earlier in this century.

The ramifications of this for American strength and influence are not good. Those nations most commonly thought to embody Western values are not replacing their own stock. This hints, of course, of shifts in military and cultural dominance in future global affairs.

One chief aspect of culture is religion. Fertility rates show that the people living in some of the strongholds of Judeo- Christian heritage and values—America and Europe—are not reproducing themselves. Consider what's happening in the world's major metropolises. Only seven of the world's twenty-five largest cities were predominantly non-Christian in 1950. It's been projected that by 2000, seventeen of the twenty-five largest cities will have mostly non-Christian populations. Nearly all those cities are strongholds of Islam, Hinduism or other non-Christian religions.[5] As for Muslims, their total fertility rate is closer to 6.0—more than three times that of industrialized nations. Christianity's biggest competitors have no qualms about bedroom-based growth programs. Neither do they have reservations about immigration, both legal and illegal, to the West.

Sovereign God, of course, can initiate a revival that would overshadow these trends. But are Christians presumptuous to wait and hope for that to happen? Is it the church or the Hindus who have inherited God's promises to Adam and Abraham to be fruitful and multiply and subdue the earth (Gen. 1:28), to become as numerous as the stars of heaven? Are Christians co-conspirators with the baby-busters of this age, or is the church exhibiting the Bible's pro-natalist (pro-birth) thrust?

The answer to the last question is nothing to be proud of: Christians are limiting their families almost as much as their secular neighbors.

The American baby boom was "largely a Catholic phenomenon," according to Allan Carlson, who has tracked changes in the American family through the erudite *The Family in America* newsletter of the Rockford Institute Center on the Family in America. Carlson notes that "non-Catholics averaged 3.15 children per woman in 1951-55 and 3.14 in 1961-65; for Catholics, the respective figures were 3.54 and 4.25." By around 1970, though, the Catholic boom had busted. During 1967 to 1971, "average expected family size among Catholics fell from 3.3 children to 2.8 in that period, a substantially greater decline than seen among Protestants."[6]

Overall, the formerly renowned Catholic fertility has fallen toward the rate of Protestants, especially the more prolific conservative Protestants. And religious fertility, as a whole, appears to have trailed the national norm, which has most certainly plunged. In recent decades, only evangelical and fundamentalist churches have demonstrated much bullishness on childbearing.[7] According to Carlson, Catholic fertility has had "unexpected resilience" in the last ten years, though some of it may be due to heavy immigration of prolific Hispanic Catholics. Mormons are the only religious group in America showing fertility rates significantly above the rest of the nation.

It appears, then, that American families claiming religious affiliation are producing two, sometimes three, babies per family. Sizable numbers are obviously having only one child or remaining barren. Most of us can remember Catholic families in the 1960s with six or eight children. Such situations were notable, but not utterly freakish. Today, when a couple is expecting even its fourth child, as my wife and I were not many years ago, the news is met with responses ranging from guarded congratulations to utter bewilderment. People who would not normally be so bold suddenly blurt, "Was this one planned?" (Yes, it was.)

The church has lost its salt in this area. It has been swept up in modern forces, some of them beyond its control.

Why Not Be a Mother?

Christian anti-natalism (attitudes against procreation) caught the attention of William H. Willimon, an assistant professor of liturgy and worship at Duke University's divinity school and a premarital counselor. Writing in 1980, he lamented the growing number of couples who considered parenthood a mere option to marriage. Asked about plans for children, couples often responded, "We really haven't gotten into that question yet," and, "Kids just don't fit into our career plans."[8]

The counselor had come face to face with the narcissistic "now" generation. It was not a pretty sight: children of convenience fast-forwarding their lives and values beyond older church tradition and teaching that linked procreation with marriage. Something was lost in the blur.

One problem is simply that it's hard to be a mother these days. Social and kin support for pregnant women and new mothers was more common in years past in Western nations, as it is today in many non-Western nations. Their own mothers or mothers-in-law would frequently be in the same village or city, willing to help with housework, cook, and care for the newborn and other siblings.

Today, in industrialized, mobile nations like the United States, it is all too common for young families to live away from their parents. Many times during a pregnancy my wife has moaned for her mother's help. And sometimes she received it, though it meant a drive of 250 miles for her mother or for us, and the help was only temporary. Other women are not even that fortunate.

In later years, older mothers need the support of their children. Traditionally, retired parents could count on the support and esteem of their nearby younger children. Now it is increasingly likely that those adult children are living out of town, absorbed in their own affairs, unable or unwilling to do any more for Mom or Pop except make sure the nursing home bills get paid. In coming years, the neglect will be even worse because there will be fewer, if any, children to drop by for a visit or provide low-level physical care. In some cases, it may be the outworking of a grim justice: grown children, having sensed the burden they were to their parents, unconsciously returning the favor by reckoning their own parents as burdens.

Modern culture, even in the stereotype it sets for women, has turned anti-natalist. In Western nations more than others, women are considered to be attractive when they are thin. By contrast, the slightest plumping drives some women to nervous fits, even to psychological disorders such as forced vomiting.

Pregnancy—both the swelling of the uterus and the weight gains that frequently linger from multiple pregnancies—contradicts this obsession with thinness. Yet in other nations, as feminist Germaine Greer notes in her book *Sex and Destiny*, a long period of multiple pregnancies is considered normal for women, and meat on the bones is found attractive. Clothing is designed accordingly. It is usually loose enough to expand during pregnancy and flexible enough to facilitate breast feeding. In America, a whole industry is built around maternity clothes. Pregnancy is a rare adventure, like a trip to the beach, that requires special garb.

Specially designed clothing also is needed almost always for a mother to breast-feed her baby. The practice has become somewhat more accepted in recent years, though it is still considered by some almost a cultic practice. It is considered best practiced in seclusion. Americans are far better acquainted with the female breast in sensual terms rather than as a nurturing part of infant care.

Against the Tide

Many other factors are working against modern maternity. Wattenberg identified several currents pushing against the traditional favor on parenting and large families. He groups them in four categories: socioeconomic, legal/technological/medical, lifestyle and values.

Socioeconomic
• Urbanization: When farmers move to the city, fertility usually declines. America's farm population is about 2.4 percent of its total, compared to about nine-

ty percent in 1790. This alone could almost account for the disappearance of those seven-baby mothers of the late 1700s.

• Education: Fertility also goes down as education for women goes up, as evidenced in the cultured Western nations afflicted by the birth dearth.

• Wealth: When wealth increases, fertility drops. Even though couples might be more financially equipped to raise children, paradoxically they shy away from it. One reason is that good pension plans available in industrialized nations take away some of the traditional incentive to have children for care in old age.

• Working women: Fertility plunges when women of childbearing age enter the work force. "In the U.S. in 1940, only seventeen percent of married women were in the labor force full or part time; today the figure is fifty-three percent. Labor economists believe rates of working women will continue to rise," Wattenberg notes.

Legal/Technological/Medical

• Abortion: The Western nations Wattenberg examined were performing an estimated six million abortions a year. The United States at that time was responsible for 1.5 million of that, or one-fourth.

The coming to market of an abortion pill suggests that abortions will increase further. In 1988, China and France sanctioned use of the French-made abortion pill, RU 486. Pro-abortionists were lobbying hard in the early 1990s to clear the way for RU 486 into the United States. Even if they fail, the pill, like other illegal drugs, probably will find its way into a black market.

• Contraception: Birth control is more widely available and more socially acceptable than ever before. And, according to Wattenberg, many couples are deadly serious about avoiding pregnancy: "Among currently married couples in the U.S. today, thirty-nine percent have at least one surgically sterile partner."

Life-style Factors
• Delayed marriage: As of 1986, age of marriage in the United States was at its highest level ever—23.1 years for women, 25.7 for men. The longer a woman stays single, the more likely she is to postpone child-bearing.

• Delay of birth of first child: Not only do couples wait longer to get married, they wait longer to have their first child. The cumulative effect is fewer children.

• Divorce: America's abnormally high divorce rates of recent decades have caused problems enough for both spouses and children. A less publicized effect of divorce, though, is that it removes women temporarily, if not permanently, from being likely candidates for motherhood.

• Decreased fertility: Wattenberg writes that "the incidence of medical factors that can make a woman infertile has increased." This figure includes the women who are trying to become pregnant at later ages and those contracting fertility- impairing venereal disease.

• Never married: The proportion of women who will never marry is expected to rise sharply, obviously hurting fertility rates.

• Homosexuality and lesbianism: It's hard to measure if the adherents to these practices have increased or simply gone public, but it seems they have increased.

• Unmarried couples: "Significant others" living together without benefit of a marriage ceremony are much less likely to procreate—which is probably for the best—but this, too, is a trend that has increased enormously since the 1960s and has suppressed fertility.

Values

• Women's liberation: Marriage, and particularly motherhood, got a bad rap from the self-ordained spokespersons for American women.

• Financial costs to raise children: Wattenberg's analysis of per capita and family income changes during recent decades concludes that "the Birth Dearth has not been caused by people having less real income to raise children." Rather, many more wives are in the work force; whenever a working wife gets pregnant, it takes her out of a job, at least temporarily, and hence reduces family income.

Even if that is not a major factor, children are a major consumption item. One estimate is that it costs $135,000 to raise a child from infancy through college. Other estimates have run much higher.

• Environmentalism: I find it hard to believe that more than a token number of people decide against having a child because of alleged overpopulation and its real or imagined effects, such as depletion of resources. "Gosh, Mary, you know another kid would further drain the earth's limited natural gas reserves, not to mention the effect on the deteriorating ozone layer. And what would the neighbors say?" But, as Wattenberg points out, the total impact of an effective population lobby has created a general climate that discourages fertility.

It comes as no surprise, then, with so many elements reinforcing the idea of procreation as a burden, that children are perceived—often accurately—as burdens when they are born and while they grow to adulthood. As we will see in the next chapter, many mothers are all too willing to distance themselves from their screaming new housemates as soon as they can. And as children approach adulthood, our culture encourages them to be unproductive burdens for longer than ever before in history.

TWO

ABANDONED PRESCHOOLERS, DORMANT TEENS

You shall have sons and daughters but they shall not be yours, for they shall go into captivity.

(Deuteronomy 28:41)

H ere's a tough one:

If you're a congressman who shares the conviction that children are a blessing, should you support legislation calling for tax-funded day care so that working mothers can afford the best possible care for their children?

Carol Polsgrove, writing in *The Progressive*, described her troubles in finding the right child care. When Ms. Polsgrove was almost ready to return to work half time, she found a place to leave her five-month-old daughter. It was at the home of a woman who cared for several toddlers, "but I was depressed by the small, dim house and the grime ground deep in the carpets and furniture."[1] She kept her daughter there for a brief time.

Later she joined a parents' cooperative staffed with part-time child-care workers. The co-op cared for eight children under two years old in what local Californians called a cottage. "Back in Kentucky, we would call it a shack. And even that shack was about to be taken away."[2] Landlord troubles, it seems.

And so it went for Ms. Polsgrove. By the end of the article, her two-year-old daughter was attending nursery school to the tune of $5,000 a year.

Her moral: Most people, even many professionals, cannot afford decent care for their children. We need a large national system of public and private child care.

But there is more to this dilemma than meets the eye. If government, or the private sector, expands the national child-care system, will it reinforce the idea that children are a blessing, or will it confirm that they are troublesome burdens to be pushed out of the way as quickly as possible? The legitimate need some mothers have for child care obscures a more central point: Is child care good for preschool kids?

Pro-Family vs. Pro-Family

Many mothers, notably single mothers, have little choice about being in the work place. Most of them need child-care help from relatives, friends or church, or perhaps financial assistance—from the government or their employer—to treat their children like the blessings they are. As for the propriety of married mothers seeking work outside the home, chapter 6 will explore the topic more fully. For now, suffice it to say that of the more than nine million preschoolers in child care, a great number of them have married mothers who do not absolutely need employment outside the home.

According to child-care advocates like Ms. Polsgrove, one answer to the problem of finding affordable, quality child care is the same answer liberals find for every other social program: Throw more money at it.

Author George Gilder, quoting former Congressman Jack Kemp, observed: "If you want more of something, subsidize it; if you want less, tax it." Commenting on the Act for Better Child Care, the Democrats' entree for their alleged "pro-family" spread during 1988, Gilder noted:

> The day-care bill will tax families that care for their own children in order to subsidize families that place their children in another's care. The more the state subsidizes the breakdown of family responsibilities, the more families will break down. But there is simply no way on earth for government to supply the love and attention and self-sacrifice that mothers spontaneously offer their children. There are not enough resources on this entire planet to raise a new generation of civilized children if mothers defect.[3]

The issue, then, is not just what mothers need, but what children need. What should our national consensus endorse to align itself with a godly concern for children: care by natural mother or care by surrogate mothers? The advocates of child care would have us believe there is no difference, or even that care away from home offers benefits to the child. Let's look closer at the effects of day care on children and see if it reflects a regard for children as blessings.

The Unspoken Damage

A distant observer might think that American women, now that they are having fewer children, would be willing to devote more time to those few children. No such luck. They are more eager than ever to dump them at child-care centers, sometimes only weeks after birth.

In 1960, less than one-fifth of married mothers with children under six worked; and as late as 1975, only one-third worked, including part-time workers. Now more than half of American women with children under age five are working—thirty-five percent are working full time, twenty percent part time.[4]

The mothers' rush to the work place escalated rapidly, probably too rapidly. Bryce Christensen, writing in *The Family in America* newsletter, compares day care to thalidomide. That prenatal drug was billed by its manufacturer as "completely safe," yet it caused massive birth defects in thousands before being taken off the market.

Day care's problems, though in some cases only speculative—as were thalidomide's initially—may well prove to be just as serious. Thalidomide was vigorously defended by its manufacturer even after problems became public. Day care, too, Christensen says, has its defenders who have tried to evade the surfacing problems and attack those who refuse to align themselves with the socialist agenda that incorporates widespread day care.[5] For example, one of Canada's leading psychologists, Otto Weininger, for many years was "unable to publish in any professional journal a watershed work on the effects of day care."[6]

While child care has been praised and occasionally criticized in the professional journals, it has rarely emerged as a public issue except as one of government funding for more of it. Meanwhile, the damage goes on.

The primary harm that day care inflicts is developmental. You don't have to be a sociologist with a Ph.D. to assess the emotional mine field that group day care represents: Your child is separated from his natural mother for most of his waking hours. He does not see the same adults over the long term because his center's staff turns over more than twice as fast as the national turnover rate. Unless the child is in an exceptional—and therefore expensive—program, he is watched by workers who in 1984 had median annual earnings of $9,200 (about $2,000 less than janitors).[7] These low-wage workers—"care-givers" is the current euphemism—have so many kids to give care to that they are understandably not as happy and devoted as a child's biological care-giver would be.

This is no fertile seed bed for emotional health. Here are some of the developmental problems specialists have found:

• Children placed in day care as infants are more likely than home-reared children "to hit, to kick, to push, to threaten, to swear, to tease and to argue."[8]

• "Repeated daily separations experienced by infants whose mothers are working full time constitute a 'risk' factor" for the development of personality.[9]

• "The mother-child bond often deteriorates when children under twelve months are placed in day care."[10]

• When there is insecure parent-infant bonding, "the child's later conduct is characterized by 'noncompliance, aggressiveness, social withdrawal and behavior problems in general.'"[11]

• Day-care children often possess "an hedonic quality—a feeling of joylessness, an inability to experience pure pleasure."[12]

• "'Children who had been in full-time child care (as infants or later) were rated by parents and teachers as having poorer work-study skills and as being less compliant' when compared to children who had been in the care of their mothers during their preschool years." The day-care kids also had poorer self-images and lower grades in grades one through three.[13]

Then there are the physical health problems. Again, common sense tells you a lot. A room full of kids sticking fingers into mouths and across dripping nostrils and smearing those fingers over commonly used toys is a greenhouse for spreading viruses and bacteria. Sure enough. Day-care centers have been linked with:

• "outbreaks of gastroenteritis caused by bacteria, viruses and parasites; bacterial meningitis [or] hepatitis A."[14]

• "outbreaks of enteric illness—diarrhea, dysentery, giardiasis and epidemic jaundice—reminiscent of the pre-sanitation days of the seventeenth century."[15]

• hemophilus influenza type B, which can lead to childhood meningitis and epiglottis.[16]

- cytomegalovirus, which can be transmitted to pregnant women and "cause birth defects affecting hearing, brain development, neuromuscular function and vision."[17]

Some—and only some—of the emotional and physical problems of day care can be minimized in higher-quality centers, but even money cannot buy another *real* mother. As William and Wendy Dreskin operated a high-quality center for three years, they noticed "how children in day care suffer from separation anxiety and depression despite competent staff." They did not like what they saw. So they closed their center.[18]

Esteemed psychiatrist and psychoanalyst Harold M. Voth describes as a "national tragedy" the large segment of working women with preschool children. Recognizing that many women are forced to work for economic reasons, Voth says others simply choose to flee the home and escape their offspring. He says

> the phenomenon reflects a massive flight from their environment which, for them, is conflict triggering....Further, they do not see the value of motherhood, and instead heed the clarion call of the feminist movement's antifamily propaganda. The negative impact of this propaganda on the personalities of their children, and ultimately upon society, defies estimation. If the trend continues, the movement will wreck our society. *No society can survive if mothers do not care for the young*, if the family does not survive. When the number of emotionally disturbed people is

greater than the number of healthy ones, the
vitality of the nation will irrevocably decline
and eventually collapse (italics added).[19]

Voth is saying that when parents reckon children as
burdens, even curses, instead of blessings, *the children indeed become a burden.* A generation marked
by emotional disturbance rather than healthy maturity,
identity, and productivity will for years burden their
parents and society rather than bless them.

The issue of providing affordable child care for
those who need it, as well as for those who merely
find it convenient, will be on the social/political
agenda for some time. It presents challenges to
Christians who believe natural family, or at second
best, church family, is the best environment for raising children. We can work through churches to meet
the child-care and financial needs of single mothers.
We can provide physical and emotional support
(including occasional child care) for those mothers
who sacrifice paid work to work as home-based
mothers. We can renew the ties between generations
so that grandparents function as a useful, meaningful
and natural part of the family child-raising and child-
care process.

If we fail to come forward with a higher way that
affirms the worth and special needs of children, the
state will be all too eager to come forward with its way.
And it will gladly hand *all* of us the bill, in the form of
higher taxes, whether we want the services or not.

Those Wonder Years: Adolescence

When I was a child, advertisements for Wonder Bread described ages one to twelve as the "wonder years," when your child develops in twelve different ways. In modern America, adolescence could be called the wonder years in another sense: when your child wonders for about eight years or longer whether or not he should grow up. When the choice is to be a consumer-oriented burden or a producer-oriented blessing, the decision is easy.

We take for granted that children need a transition period between childhood and adulthood, roughly between ages twelve and twenty. During this interim, they are getting more education and training for a career and learning the ropes of courtship so they can eventually be a responsible marriage partner.

This delayed adulthood is unusual by historical standards. Prior to 1800, youth was the period when children prepared for adult life. It was a long transition, but its organization was such that the children could see their progress into adulthood. This changed in the modern era.

> During the nineteenth century childhood was extended into something called adolescence, when teenagers were left to concentrate on the tensions and stresses of those years of growth. Thus, these youngsters were excused from participation in the larger society while they concentrated on personal growth.[20]

In many societies throughout history, as in some cases still today, children became adults in their early teens. This often would happen at one juncture, usually marked by a ceremony. The Jews, for example, still hold a bar mitzvah service for boys on their thirteenth birthday and bas mitzvah for girls turning twelve or thirteen. These rites designate their joining the adult community and assuming the responsibilities of adulthood.

In contrast, the Western world has the longest period of adolescence in history. Why? Much of it is due to the ongoing industrial revolution. The training required to enable young people to become self-supporting in the industrialized nations cannot (or will not) be fulfilled by most parents, as it naturally is in agricultural societies. Apprenticeships outside the home have become rare, and where they survive they still involve a foundation of formal education. The usual alternative to apprenticeship is going to school, which now means until at least age seventeen or eighteen, increasingly until twenty-one or twenty-two for those pursuing higher education, and even longer for post-graduate specialties.

As this change has set in during the last one hundred years or so, it has drastically altered the balance of how children could be a physical blessing to families. No longer are the youthful years spent canning food, crafting clothes, fishing at sea, plowing fields, harvesting and so on. For most kids, those years are devoted to playing and studying, too often in that order.

There is no use in lamenting such changes, especially considering that the accompanying progress has given society more than it has lost. But note two points: *Christians need to understand that this is one of several developments that undermine the Biblical valuation of children as God's blessings.* Children's contributions as producers for family and society are postponed several years. They tend to be a financial burden for almost twice as long as before, while the costs of education make that delay much more expensive than it ever would have been in the past.

The prosperity and materialism of Western culture has exaggerated the shift from work to education and recreation for teenagers. In other words, the work ethic has gone the way of the slide rule. Teens from poor and lower-middle-class families still take paying jobs; many of the rest don't, except perhaps during summers. The contributions of most students of any age to household chores are probably far less than what they should be. Even when parents are cognizant of that lack, they may spend most of their administrative energies coaxing homework out of their children who are understandably bored with school. It is no surprise that pre-adolescents and adolescents are hardly perceived as blessings.

When John and Peter were growing up, they had plenty of chores. Their friends felt sorry for them because the brothers were running errands, weeding the garden, and taking out garbage. As they aged, they mowed grass or did other jobs.

> But when the boys reached adulthood, they were better off than their childhood playmates who had been less industrious. They earned more money and had more job satisfaction. They had better marriages and closer relationships with their children. They were healthier and lived longer. Most of all they were happier.[21]

John and Peter were part of a forty-year Harvard University study that traced 456 teenage boys from inner-city Boston and compared them at middle age. One dominant result from the study was that

> regardless of intelligence, family income, ethnic background or amount of education, those who had worked as boys, even at simple household chores, enjoyed happier and more productive lives than those who had not.[22]

The parents of those boys who had worked at chores understood that children at even a young age can, and should, bless their families by doing at least some work. Formal education was not so great a responsibility that it had to detract from the productive side of life. Those parents were simply bringing up children the way they had been brought up: to respect the work ethic. The fruits for their children were prosperity, stability, and happiness as adults.

Compare that mentality with a group of about four hundred eight-to-ten-year-olds surveyed at a Pennsylvania theme park in 1986. Nearly half of them said they wanted to grow up to be athletes and entertainers. More than half of them would decline the chance to be president, citing that job as "too much work" or "too dangerous." Only thirty-seven percent said they wanted to be president; twenty-eight percent of that group "wanted the job because it would make them rich and famous."[23]

Easy money, fame, and low risk—these dreams will not last long in motivating young men and women to work for themselves and their families year after year, initially at low wages, forever in obscurity. One wishes that such whimsy was merely the amusing fantasy that comes with career planning by eight-to-ten-year-olds. Unfortunately, for too many the fog lingers into the adult years.

In her book *The Postponed Generation,* Susan Littwin interviewed many young adults coming of age in the 1970s and 1980s. The results were depressing. Brought up with the affluence of middle-class America in the 1950s and 1960s, they expected the same and more—good salary, prestigious work in their college major, home ownership. Too often there was no job, or at least nothing attractive, waiting on the other side of graduation.

Some graduates hung around their parents' home, waiting for the right job, flirting with graduate school, whatever it took to avoid full-fledged adulthood and all its nasty responsibilities. Marriage was always an option, but there seemed to be no urgency to jump into it or to maintain it if it did not coast from day to day. The book's subtitle put it in a nutshell: "Why America's Grown-up Kids Are Growing Up Later."

Ms. Littwin recounted a career change workshop at an urban university. The group, reviewing a session on assertiveness training, sifts through a pile of material. A woman finds a list of "developmental tasks" that offends her.

"This is from some other world," she protests, exasperated. "According to this, a person in her late twenties should be establishing a permanent relationship with a mate, a home and a life's work. I'm nowhere near that. Neither is anybody else I know in their late twenties." Everyone seems to agree with her. Those may have been realistic goals once upon a time, but now, in the eighties, they are clearly impossible. The review of assertiveness training is dropped.[24]

Welcome to America in the late twentieth century. Those children who aren't ripped out of the womb and thrown away face an increasing likelihood of being parked in damaging institutions for large portions of their formative years. Their parents go into debt giving them free room and board for the next decade or two, demanding little labor in return. Parents give their children more years than ever to "find themselves," only to discover that in their mid-twenties they still lack full identity. Parents should not be perplexed to find that their indulgence of sometimes excessive schooling and work avoidance has left their adult children confused, unemployed, and single.

Of course, many parents and their children do not fit this mold. But while many young adults have escaped these trends, more and more find themselves snared in the elastic twilight zone of adolescence. This promises not a harvest of blessings, but of handicapped burdens.

Before we examine further the fruits of modern social trends and how they are sabotaging the traditional Christian favor on procreation and large families, let's examine the Biblical foundations. In spite of the changes wrought by the industrial age, there remains a solid blueprint for ordering the family by an alternate value system. Children *can* be a blessing, even in the midst of this turmoil.

PART 1

THE FOUNDATION

THREE

BE FRUITFUL
AND MULTIPLY

"For you will spread abroad to the right and to the left. And your descendants will possess nations, and they will resettle the desolate cities."

Isaiah 54:3

At last the rancher had it all. God had blessed him with seven sons and three daughters who maintained households on his sprawling ranch. More than ten thousand animals—sheep, oxen, donkeys, and camels—grazed over hundreds of acres. In addition to the help he received from his sons and daughters, he employed dozens of hired hands. It's written that this guy was the greatest of all the men in his part of the world.

Then, suddenly, his bubble burst. A strange incident wiped out all of his sheep. Bands of marauders stole the rest of his herds. To top it off, a freak accident killed all ten of his children. In the course of all this violence, all but four of his servants also perished.

"The Lord gave and the Lord has taken away," said the rancher, who maintained his humility even in the midst of calamity. "Blessed be the name of the Lord."

Years passed, and the rancher and his wife—not believers in birth control—found themselves again with seven sons and three daughters. In the land where they lived, there was no government-sponsored Aid to Families With Dependent Children, as in the United States today. There were no food stamps. There was no subsidized housing. There were no public schools to educate those ten children. Worst of all, there was no television to act as automatic babysitter.

In a fix like this, what's an aging parent to do?

Rejoice!

Rejoicing over such circumstances was natural for this rancher—Job, of Bible fame—because there was no doubt in his mind that the addition of children was a blessing from God.

But times change. How many people today, even those of wealth, could raise ten children, lose them, and as they move toward their retirement years, count themselves rewarded when they become saddled with the task of raising ten more?

The difference between then and now that comes to mind for most of us is that culture has changed drastically since Job's day. Boys were apprenticed at an early age into their father's occupation; girls were trained to be mothers and homemakers. Children's contributions to household maintenance and the family vocation of ranching, farming, or fishing were tangible and necessary. Until children reached adulthood, they amounted to free labor and, in some cases, management trainees for the family business.

True enough—such is not the case with children in today's industrialized nations. But there's something deeper here, something more profound about the value of children than their mere utility. Job's appraisal of children reflects mainstream Biblical thought: *Children are an unmitigated blessing from God.* The idea is not some obscure Jewish proverb. It is not fodder for a bogus Mother's Day sermon geared to manipulate mothers to continue their round-the-clock restaurant/laundry/chauffeur service for yet another year.

The Bible's exaltation of fertility is part of God's divine plan for the family, the community, and the world. It was no odd concept to Job, nor to others throughout most of history. Yet today, the thought of a large family is apt to stir visions of poverty and ignorance: An immigrant Catholic family selling vegetables in New York, struggling to get by. A black woman on welfare, with no man around, supporting six children in a crowded housing project. An Appalachian mountain family, fighting winter's bite, with unemployed father and countless barefoot kiddies huddled around a wood-burning stove in a drafty shack.

It does no good to deny that these images represent real situations. Christian parents, however, as spiritual men and women, are challenged to think beyond physical appearances, especially when Scripture offers hope for something better. In later chapters we'll see there are principles, with Biblical support, that hold the key for growing families and growing communities to transcend poverty. But first, let's examine some of the basic Scripture passages regarding procreation and God's general plan for population.

A Tall Order

God's first command to man was a big one: "Be fruitful and multiply, and fill the earth, and subdue it; and rule over the fish of the sea and over the birds of the sky, and over every living thing that moves on the earth" (Gen. 1:28).

It's far too rash to dismiss this command, given to Adam, as one needed simply to get the ball rolling as far as getting some warm bodies spread around the globe, taming some useful animals, and cultivating some land. God put no expiration date on His order. It was not void east of the Rockies.

Nothing in the New Testament, when population and civilization were already well advanced (by Genesis standards), indicated there would come a day when man needed to apply brakes to Genesis 1:28. Though Paul expressed reservations about the married state in general (in the context of the expected imminent Second Coming, 1 Cor. 7), he also wrote more specifically to Timothy that "women shall be preserved (or saved) through the bearing of children" (1 Tim. 2:15). Later chapters will examine these New Testament passages more closely.

Some expositors say that Gen. 1:28 is not so much God giving a command as it is Him bestowing a blessing. I have no problem with this interpretation; in fact, it probably adds needed balance to what for some is a controversy over whether the use of contraception is sinful for Christians. Still, as a blessing, it's clear that God joyfully anticipated man's *filling* the earth, not his elaborate attempts to choke back population.

Have you ever seen bees swarming around their hive? Or ants swarming when a lawnmower lops off the top of their hill? Or flying insects swarming around a porch light in the summer? Well, God is interested in people swarms. After Noah's family left the ark, "God blessed Noah and his sons and said to them, 'Be fruitful and multiply, and fill the earth'" (Gen. 9:1). He repeated the order in 9:7: "Be fruitful and multiply; populate the earth abundantly and multiply in it." The second part of the verse means, literally, to swarm in the earth.

Then came Abram. The Bible tells us he was a righteous man, his righteousness reckoned according to his faith. But as he grew older, his faith was tested almost to the breaking point, it seemed to him. That strange God had told him to leave his father's house and homeland and travel to this new country, a land linked to this God's promises. So far, so good. But what about this business of having descendants who would be as numerous as the dust of the earth (Gen. 13:16) and the stars (15:5)?

Years went by without getting descendant number one. Finally, his wife Sarai blamed it on the Lord. "*Please* go in to my maid," she begged Abram. "Perhaps I shall obtain children through her."

Abram conceded. He was getting up there in years, and so was Sarai. He conceived Ishmael through the maidservant Hagar. Yet even this son, conceived in lieu of God's promise, was to receive promises similar to those granted Abraham's chosen line. God told

Hagar her descendants would "be too many to count" (Gen. 16:10). God said of Ishmael He would "multiply him exceedingly" and "make him a great nation" (Gen. 17:20).

Abram was eighty-six at Ishmael's birth. Thirteen years later, when Abram was ninety-nine, God was at it again. He was still carrying on about multitudes of children and grandchildren—only it was Sarai, not Hagar, who remained God's choice for matriarch. Then one day there was all this rigmarole—perhaps it seemed a little overboard to Abram at the time— when that majestic Deity was speaking to him and he fell to the ground:

> As for Me, behold, My covenant is with you,
> And you shall be the father of a multitude of
>   nations.
> No longer shall your name be called Abram,
> But your name shall be Abraham;
> For I will make you the father of a multitude
>   of nations.
> And I will make you exceedingly fruitful, and
>   I will make nations of you, and kings shall
>   come forth from you (Gen. 17:4-6).

The promised son, Isaac, finally arrived through Sarai. Only by that point, God had renamed her Sarah, or "princess," a fitting title for a mother of "kings."

God was certainly clear enough with Abraham that he was to be the father of a multitude and that he was to count it a blessing. But He didn't stop there. The Bible records the affirmation of the promises to the next two generations. When Rebekah, Isaac's bride-to-be, was leaving her home to meet Isaac, her family gave her a blessing of fertility:

"May you, our sister,
Become thousands of ten thousands,
And may your descendants possess
The gate of those who hate them"
(Gen. 24:60).

Isaac received the same promises of multiplication that God gave to his father (26:4 and 26:24). When Isaac sent his son Jacob to Paddan-aram to find a wife, he passed on the blessing: "And may God Almighty bless you and make you fruitful and multiply you, that you may become a company of people" (28:3).

As Jacob dreamed of the angels on the ladder, God confirmed the promise that his descendants would be like the dust of the earth, spreading out in all directions, and that through him all families would be blessed (28:14). Many years later God reminded him of the promise, including, as well, part of the Genesis 1:28 command: "Be fruitful and multiply; a nation and a company of nations shall come from you, and kings shall come forth from you" (35:11).

God even expanded that promise. As the Israelites were leaving Egypt en route to subdue Canaan, God promised them long life and no miscarriages—in other words, conditions for a population explosion, notes Gary North in *The Dominion Covenant*.[1] And this word came to a people who had already experienced history's greatest population boom.

This same growth potential was evident in the life of the rancher, Job. He lost all his children and wealth, and his health was afflicted. When God decided to bless him, he received ten children, more wealth than he had before, and a long life. North observes: "In short, he was given the capital he needed to begin once again to exercise dominion over the earth as a godly family man: *tools, children and time*"[2] (author's italics). Tools (or wealth), children, and time—they represented capital in Job's day, and they should today. Large (and sometimes prosperous) families, walking patiently in covenant with God, were eventually to take Canaan. There is no reason to think families of the same mold cannot prosper, multiply, and exert godly influence in modern states. The Genesis 1:28 mandate to subdue and rule over the earth is still valid.

But, Lord, You Promised!

Sometimes God is not content merely to make promises to test His people. He allows circumstances to become truly difficult so that the miracle-working side of His personality (and perhaps His sense of humor) will be abundantly clear.

A vast portion of the fifty chapters of Genesis is absorbed with the saga of three great patriarchs—Abraham, Isaac and Jacob. Each was told that God would bring forth a multitude from him. Yet what did these supposed superdads have in common for many years? A barren wife!

The childless wife was horrid enough in this Hebrew culture that prized offspring, especially sons. Barrenness, in fact, was grounds for divorce. How much more frustrating to know that the sovereign

God of your fathers had promised to bring forth great nations from you, yet you and the Mrs. couldn't even get as far as morning sickness.

God uses dilemmas such as these to draw people's hearts to Him. He causes them to live by faith when it becomes painfully obvious that answers cannot be wrought in the flesh. Sarah, for example, laughed when she overheard the prophecy that she and her ninety-nine-year-old husband were to have a child within a year (Gen. 18:12). But in the midst of her hopelessness, God came in. "By faith Sarah herself received ability to conceive, even beyond the proper time of life, since she considered Him faithful who had promised" (Heb. 11:11). Faith, too, has an obvious role for the Christian couple thwarted by barrenness or intimidated by the prospect of additional children when money, time, and patience are already in short supply.

It's no accident that God chose the area of procreation to demonstrate His miraculous power. That mysterious transfer of the seed, with all its potential for life and increase, manifests in the flesh the creative, fruit-bearing nature of God the Father. His Word records miraculous conceptions not only for the patriarchs' wives Sarah (Gen. 21:1,2), Rebekah (Gen. 25:21), and Rachel (Gen. 30:22), but also for Manoah's wife (Judges 13:3-24), the Shunammite woman (2 Kin. 4:14-17), Hannah (1 Sam. 1:19,20), Elizabeth (Luke 1:24,25,36,37,58), and Mary (Matt. 1:18,20). These eight instances reconfirm in precious ways what God says through the psalmist: "He makes the barren woman abide in the house as a joyful mother of children" (Ps. 113:9).

For these eight, the fruit of the womb was a *reward* for, among other things, the faith exercised by parents who believed God was still in the miracle business. It was a *blessing* for those who anticipated God's multiplication of the Hebrew nation into one that would fill the earth in fulfillment of the promises to the patriarchs. That same blessing and reward are just as rich today. Isaiah prophesied that there will be no end to the increase of God's kingdom (Is. 9:7). Accordingly, Christian parents should understand that God's blessing of fertility is one method by which He extends His reign on earth.

God the Multiplier

Deuteronomy 28, a chapter detailing God's blessings and curses, states overwhelmingly that increase is good. This chapter sets out the blessings for the Hebrews if they will obey God's commands and gives a much longer list of curses, should they choose to reject God's law. Twice God mentions the blessing of abounding in "the offspring of your body" (28:4,11), and each time the blessing is lumped together with other increases of herds and crops. Increase is increase in God's economy. And He wants it known He is "the man behind the scene."

Most couples today want to modify the Deuteronomy 28 blessing package. They're plenty willing to order a big blessing sandwich, but on their terms: "Give me increase in herds and crops (or salary, cars and stock prices), but hold off with the kids. And a bigger house would be nice, but just don't stuff it with boisterous little monsters who'll smear their grimy hands on the new living room sofa."

Those who reject children—whether by abortion, voluntary barrenness, or the inordinate limitation of family size—are rejecting the Deuteronomy 28 blessing. They are, by default, aligning themselves with the Deuteronomy 28 curse of a closed womb and abducted children. They are redefining Scriptural blessings and curses according to their own preferences.

This is far from the heart of our pro-life, or *procreative*, God. His first book of recorded history sets in motion a torrential momentum of His people filling the earth and training their sights on ruling over the promised land. Even by the time of the exodus from Egypt, the fulfilled promise was swarming over the land. From the patriarchs' once-barren wives had sprung millions of people (600,000 men and their families), multiplying in the unlikely hothouse of a four-hundred-year slavehood in the sands of Egypt. No modern trend or reasoning can invalidate God's linkage of increase with blessing.

Faith for Growth

Endorsing population growth in this age contradicts the many dire warnings about overpopulation. Such warnings are neither new to this century, nor very accurate. They emerge from a world view lacking faith that God has made available to His creation the resources, creativity, and planning to accommodate the needs of food, medicine, employment, and so on that come with continual growth. The secular overpopulation theme rests upon godless self-reliance, ignoring a coming day of final judgment by hoping to prolong a comfortable earthly civilization for eternity. This message of pessimism and selfishness, by its very nature, must regard marginal children as burdens. Chapter 9 examines it more closely.

There is always a temptation to think that the Old Testament insights to family and procreation represent an extremist perspective—a fragment of ancient history, applicable for a mere handful of people. We live in an era that values the immediate above the past, the "experts" above the front-line workers. We may suppose that our age's commonly accepted wisdom about children far outdistances any source as dated as the Bible.

Yet a look at the Hebrew family in the next chapter will show that Old Testament standards for family and procreation offer much for today's Christian family. It is a model that has been virtually discarded by today's sophisticated, anti-child cultures. As with any major diversion from God's order, serious consequences can be expected if societies tolerate and encourage disobedience to God's family guidelines. The first fruits—divorce, infanticide, genocidal levels of abortion and state-sponsored attacks on procreation—are already in our midst. Christians must dip into the wealth of their heritage and sow toward the opposite kind of harvest.

FOUR

THE HEBREW FAMILY

> *"And the Lord will make you abound*
> *in prosperity, in the offspring of your*
> *body and in the offspring of your beast*
> *and in the produce of your ground, in*
> *the land which the Lord swore to your*
> *fathers to give you."*
>
> (Deuteronomy 28:11)

When you hear the word "masterpiece," what do you think of? Works such as the Mona Lisa probably come to mind. A masterpiece of art is that creation where color, strokes, textures, contrast, and theme blend together in a marvelous way so that the whole is greater than the sum of the parts.

Philosopher George Santayana described the family as "one of nature's masterpieces." He was right in calling it a masterpiece. He was wrong about the master.

Sovereign God, not nature, is the creator. Family, God's pulsating masterpiece, is a special blend of personalities and passions, of youth and old age, of birth and death. Family is the crazy crucible where two adults are reduced to one, the one brings forth many, and those spouses-turned-parents become permanently altered in ways too profound and (it is hoped) too wonderful for words to describe. Family is a whole that far exceeds the sum of its components.

Psalm 68:6 says God places the solitary in families—a recognition that family is good, that the individual without family loses some identity, and that family, contrary to what homosexuals profess, typically consists of more than just two adults. Because family is God's masterpiece, it is important to see how the Scriptural blueprint for this lasting work included procreation as a prominent part of the design.

A Bulwark of Flesh and Blood

The Hebrew family packed a punch. The Encyclopedia Judaica said the emphasis on the family

> had the result of making the Jewish home the most vital factor in the survival of Judaism and the preservation of the Jewish way of life, much more than the synagogue or school. It was also a major factor for moral purity....*The powerful bond which united parents and children in one bond with mutual responsibilities and mutual consideration made it a bulwark of Judaism able to withstand all stresses from without and from within*[1] (italics added).

Children, then, played a crucial role in the dynamics of Hebrew families, including the perpetuation of their faith. It would be difficult to separate the triad—children-family-religion—because each element would wither without the other.

Modern families, even Christian ones, rarely function with this kind of intensity and purpose. One reason they fail as a stress-resistant "bulwark" is that parents lack the conviction of the Hebrew family that fertility is blessing, that children are a gift from God, to be desired and cherished.

While the world discards these ideas as antiquated patriarchalism, Christians must recapture them. This era, regarding children as little more than the by-products of intercourse, has yielded legal abortion, rising illegitimacy, multiple remarriages, record numbers of single-parent households, and a sordid array of accompanying psychopathologies—elements foreign to the Hebrew family.

Families called to be the light of the world amidst this darkness of family disintegration need to start beaming. They should broadcast an example that, like the Hebrew prototype, shows the pro-child family to be a bulwark and a haven—for the individual and the cultivation of faith—amidst the tempest of social upheaval. Let's drop back to Old Testament times to examine the family blessing, the family name/lineage, and an eye-opening philosophy of family planning. These three elements illustrate the importance of procreation in the Hebrew representation of God's masterpiece.

The Family Blessing

We've seen from Deuteronomy 28 that God does not distinguish between the objects of increase when He sends His blessing. In his study *Israel: Its Life and Culture*, Johannes Pedersen said God's blessing is

> the same strength which manifests itself in the power to found a large family and in the power to make everything flourish round one. In both cases the blessing consists in the power of fertility; fertility in the family, in the field and in the herd.[2]

Deuteronomy 28, listing the manifold blessings of fertility, describes the dream life for the Jew of that age. None of those blessings, including children, had to be sought. God said if His people were obedient, the blessings would *come upon them and overtake them* (28:2).

Seeing children as blessings as the old Hebrews did is difficult, partly because life is not as vulnerable as it once was. In Old Testament times, knowledge of health and disease was sparse. Sicknesses that can be routinely treated now would have taken lives in those days. Childbirth was without the pharmaceutical and technological wonders that are common in today's maternity wards. Now, in the industrialized nations, medicine has eradicated many fatal illnesses and provided cures for others. Medical science even can help some barren women to conceive.

Furthermore, ancient Israel had to fight the Amorites and Hittites just to survive. But in America, we do not have to fear brutal attacks by the

Mexabites or the Canadabites, wiping out a year's crops and ravaging women and children.

In short, we take for granted that adults will have all the healthy children they need, and that those children will live long lives. If one couple fails to reproduce, no sweat—others will take their place. Why care about whether God's blessing is evident in any one particular family?

Many couples do care, but their number is shrinking. *Newsweek* magazine reported in 1986 that the percentage of childless couples had doubled in the last few decades. The couples interviewed for this cover story were mostly affluent and well-educated. Yet they were ignorant with regard to carrying anything resembling a family blessing or living with any vision beyond their own meager lifespans. Whatever material blessing had fallen their way was coveted strictly for their own consumption.

Noah Appleton, for instance, a forty-three-year-old car dealer in Houston, lived at one of the city's most prestigious addresses. "This is one of the biggest reasons why we don't want children," he said shamelessly, speaking of his condominium, seventeen floors above the bustling traffic. "If we had them, we certainly couldn't live here."

Wife Janet said most of their friends were also childless, and they all enjoyed the luxury of unplanned adventures. "We've made our choice for freedom and spontaneity," she said. The couple's rejection of fertility extended even to their Abyssinian cats, which had been neutered and declawed.[3]

What sort of trade had car dealer Noah Appleton made? He bypassed children and perhaps life in the suburbs to gain an affluent, child-free condo. He and his wife swapped the satisfaction and permanence of building a posterity for the empty transience of "freedom and spontaneity." The Appletons were "free" from child-care responsibilities and related expenses; they were also free from the profound fulfillment that comes with bringing a new life into the world and seeing it blossom. In short, they were free of family blessing in the traditional sense.

The Appletons' coveting of sterility and pleasure, their voluntary severance from future generations, is antithetical to the Hebrew family system. In it, "the blessing is tantamount to the continued existence of the family, because the Israelite lives in the family. It is expressed by the term that a man gets a house."[4]

The Hebrew phrase *bet av*, or "house of a father," does not refer to a building. House means the family that proceeds from the father—his household. The father's identity, as well as that of his wife and children, is bound up in his house. Pedersen wrote that the father's blessing is completely dependent upon a son's being established in a house; the son fully comes into his own house when he occupies the father's place of authority and responsibility.[5]

To fail to have children, or for sons to fail to have children, therefore, is the destruction of the house. Identity loses meaning. The age-old family blessing suddenly terminates. Pedersen wrote "to 'beget children unto Death' is the same as to 'labour in vain' (Is. 65:23). He who has no progeny labours in vain; all the energy he uses in this life he pours into the void."[6]

Rabbinical writings took keen notice of couples who voluntarily or involuntarily had no children:

> R. Eliezer went so far as to regard the man who does not marry and shirks the duty of rearing children as equivalent to a murderer (Tosef., Yev. 8:4). The Mishnah (Yev. 6:6) lays it down as a duty to procreate, in accordance with Genesis 1:28, "Be fruitful and multiply," the minimum number of children for its fulfillment being two....So essentially was this regarded as the purpose of marriage that according to the same Mishnah not only was a man permitted, but even enjoined, to divorce his wife after ten years of barrenness.[7]

It's also common to think of a family blessing in strictly material terms. An inheritance of cash, real estate, antiques, and jewels is easy to chalk up as a blessing, a big blessing. This is not an inappropriate way to view it, but there is more involved than spending power. Abraham, for example, fully understood the nature of inheritance and its implications for progeny. Author Gary North highlights that, when God promised Abraham (then still called Abram) a "great reward" (Gen. 15:1), Abram's immediate concern was his lack of children.

> He knew that the protection and favor of God accompany a calling before God. This meant that Abraham's capital assets would now be administered within an explicit covenantal framework. Who, then, would be the heir of these assets? Who would carry on the faithful

administration of Abram's capital? Abram clearly understood the long-term nature of property under a covenant. *Capital is to be used faithfully, expanded and directed into the hands of one who will continue the faithful administration of the assets.* Capital is primarily familistic capital [8] (italics added).

As will be shown in future chapters, stewardship of wealth is a critical, down-to-earth element of the family blessing. Awareness of future generations motivates parents to earn and save and give, both for their own benefit and that of their children. It also motivates them to train children who will be even better earners, savers, and givers, for they are trustees of the blessing—in both a material and spiritual sense—that God posits in families. Not only the foolishness and sin of any one generation, but also the voracious appetite of the state's inheritance tax, are always lurking, ready to erode a family's moral and physical capital.

The Family Lineage

Perpetuating the family name is an idea that has almost been relegated to the ash can of history. Divorce and remarriage are so rampant that one hardly knows what surname to ascribe to many women and children.

And then there is the practice by which married women hyphenate their maiden name with their husband's name. Imagine if everyone adopted this practice and maintained it indefinitely. There would be an exponential increase in surnames—that is, a doubling of names (two, four, eight, sixteen and so on)—with every generation's wedding vows. Just signing a check or filling out a job application would present a major challenge in penmanship.

More serious than hyphenating names, though, is some women's refusal to assume their husband's surname. "Liberated" women who shun their mate's name are proclaiming more than they realize. They are symbolically flouting the Bible's truth that two are made one in marriage. They also are distancing themselves publicly from the esteemed role God desires them to have in extending the lineage into which they have been grafted. This would be sacrilege by Old Testament standards. Even though Hebrews did not pass on surnames as we do today for many generations, a son might reflect a father's name by being called Isaac ben-David (Isaac, son of David). The main thrust is that Hebrews highly valued continuity in the family lines.

A *Parade* magazine article about wives' keeping their own names mentioned only briefly the potential disappointment of grandparents who realize their family name will not be carried on.[9] The reader is left to assume that the current generation of marrying adults, more enlightened than their parents, has no greater worry in the matter than to calm the anguish of the fuddy-duddy elders.

Indeed, it is hard for us to realize how little we appreciate the force and sanctity behind the Hebrew value of the family line. The Israelite, Pedersen wrote, desires sons more than anything else on this earth. It is his desire to live which demands them; for the son bears his name, in him his life and soul live continually. The progeny, the "seed," is identical with the name. "For as the new heavens and the new earth, which I will make, shall remain before me, saith Yahweh, so shall your seed and your name remain" (Is. 66:22).[10]

By the same token, extermination of the name, especially Israel as a collective name, was equated with annihilation. In their requests for protection, the Israelites sometimes prodded God with the horrifying idea that their name might vanish if He didn't get them out of their current fix. Knowing they were God's chosen people, they boldly linked their name with the representation of God's name on the earth (Josh. 7:9). Just as confidently did the Israelites desire to see the names of their enemies blotted out (Deut. 7:24; 9:14; 12:3; Is. 14:22).[11]

On a personal level, one's past generations may include an embarrassing lineup of drunkards, sluggards, and the like—so much that one wishes to distance himself from his immediate heritage rather than continue it. The sentiment is understandable, but consider Jesus. His lineage is peppered with adultery and incest, yet the Gospel of Matthew prominently kicks off with a record of His forefathers. We can still take pride in a unique physical heritage and certainly in our shared spiritual heritage, which is rich in the broader blessing of God's covenant with His people.

If the past and present worth of the name means nothing to the modern individual, it follows that continuation of the name is likewise meaningless. You cannot impart what you don't realize you have. The high rate of illegitimate births in our culture reflects the attitude of men and women who have no sense of their own family name and no concern that their offspring receive the gift of secure family identity.

The challenge to the Christian parents is, therefore, enormous. They are to walk with the vision of their forefathers, realizing that the family name can signify a personalized embodiment of God's physical and spiritual blessings. Its perpetuation is no small matter.

The Wife: God's Vehicle for Blessing

With such a high premium placed on family continuity, the Hebrew wife was esteemed. The impetus to bear children and therefore help her husband extend his name and pass on his blessing in no way reflected a lower status for her. Rather, childbirth was the very thing that exalted and fulfilled a Hebrew woman. When barren, she had to do whatever it took to get children for her husband.

The demand for progeny, in fact, was so great that polygamy was fully accepted in old Israel. Eventually, the Hebrews discarded polygamy in favor of monogamy, and the New Testament has codified this standard for Christians. The importance for us is to see that Old Testament-era approval of multiple wives or concubines may have demonstrated God's concern with filling the earth with His chosen people, as He commanded in Genesis 1:28.

And what a demonstration it was. Things that were normal within the old Hebrew harems are enough to make today's soap operas and true-life tales of surrogate parenthood seem tame by comparison.

For example, it was not uncommon for the men of old Israel to turn to slave women to help expand the family when the wife (or wives) proved unfruitful. These were no slinking-around, hush-hush affairs, above all avoiding the telltale evidence of pregnancy. On the contrary, it was no-holds-barred breeding. The Bible records such roles for Hagar, Sarah's maidservant, and Bilhah and Zilpah, who were servants to Jacob's wives. Their stories illustrate how deeply ingrained in Sarah, Rachel, and Leah was the desire to extend their husbands' families and how it obviously had the stamp of social approval.

When Sarah, then still called Sarai, directs Abraham to go to Hagar (Gen. 16:2), the frustrated wife says, "Perhaps I shall obtain children through her." Rachel, sharing the same problem with Jacob, points her husband toward Bilhah with the same hope for vicarious motherhood (Gen. 30:3). Even though Jacob's other wife, Leah, gives birth to six sons, once she has ceased childbearing, she gives Zilpah to Jacob for the hope of more children.

The wives didn't have to ask about the lipstick on the collar—they knew where it originated. This is not to say they were totally selfless. For example, after Bilhah gives birth, Rachel claims the son for her own (Gen. 30:6).

A further emphasis on the importance of continuing the man's family line is found in the Deuteronomy 25 regulations for the so-called levirate marriage. If you're one who's found the best way to relate to brothers- or sisters-in-law is to maintain residences in different cities—preferably on opposite coasts—the requirements of levirate marriage may sound like hell's most devious torture.

This law provides for the case of a husband dying before his wife has produced a son. The brother of the deceased is to enter into a levirate marriage so that the woman can bear a son for the sake of her deceased husband *"that his name may not be blotted out from Israel"* (Deut. 25:6). It matters not whether the hearts of the two spontaneous spouses are fluttering from true love or wrenching revulsion. In the eyes of the Lawgiver, this was the greatest service the brother and widow could perform for their departed relative: to continue his name. Even with her husband gone, the focus of the Hebrew wife's purpose is to prevent her beloved's house from vanishing.

Genesis 38 provides a case study. Judah's son Er dies after marrying Tamar. Judah orders another son, Onan, to fulfill his duty for his brother. Cruel Onan enters into conjugal relations with Tamar, only to finish the act with the withdrawal method of birth control. In doing so, he disobeys his father and God's law. He pays with his life. (A more detailed examination of this passage in relation to the morality of contraception is presented in the next chapter.)

With two husbands dead, Tamar is beginning to look like big-time bad luck. However, her story does not end with the death of the second brother. She is told to wait for the third brother, Shelah, to grow up. So she waits. But Shelah, perhaps lacking the tolerance of a few of today's movie stars for older women, manages to weasel out of being presented to her. Enough already, says Tamar. She may be losing her youth, but not her feminine wiles. So she lays a snare for the next best candidate—father Judah—by posing as a prostitute. It works, and she conceives.

As manipulative and perverse as Tamar may seem to our civilized sensibilities, "Israelitic women have looked up to her as an example, a woman who knew how to show endurance and cunning and set aside all other considerations in order to attain the great victory, namely to give the husband progeny."[12]

Indeed, that "great victory" of giving birth was sometimes regarded by the woman as more valuable than her own life. When Jephthah vows to the Lord that he will sacrifice *or* (also translated *and*) offer as a burnt offering the first thing that comes out of his door upon returning from a victorious battle, he is greeted at home by his daughter. Some commentators suggest that her perpetual virginity would be the fulfillment of the vow, but the text more strongly indicates she died at the hand of her father. Whatever the case, she does not try to escape her father's vow, but makes one request: to retreat to the mountains for two months and mourn. Why? Not for her life, but over her virginity (Judges 11:37).

God's Planned Parenthood

Civil libertarians defending pornography and homosexuality often gripe that Christians want to "impose" their values on what consenting adults wish to do in privacy. The complainants should look at Orthodox Jewish law concerning *tarat mishpacha*, or family purity. They'd discover some real intrusions into what goes on behind closed doors.

Jewish law prohibits sexual intercourse during the five days of menstruation and the seven days following it. After this abstinence of at least twelve days, the husband (and ideally the wife) is eager for the good time that has been on the back burner for two weeks or more. Something akin to a honeymoon excitement should be in the air. The husband's sperm count will be high. And most importantly, the wife emerges from this period at her monthly point of fertility.

This is God's version of planned parenthood.

Christians are not bound to follow the letter of this Old Testament law, of course. But they would be naive to think it was pure accident that the juxtaposition of God's law and His specially designed cycle for woman so strongly favors fertility. The Creator obviously had something in mind.

As for the "honeymoon" aspect of this timing, Dr. Mayer Eisenstein, the son of an Orthodox rabbi, downplays it:

> I feel it is much too narrow a view of Jewish family life to talk about the periodic abstinence in the context of love. For love does not have a very high priority in Jewish life. We talk about duty and obligation....The conjugal act is the duty of the husband, not his right. It is his duty just as it is his duty to provide his wife with food, clothing and shelter; so he must provide her with *onah*, which is translated as the conjugal act. It is the wife who can sue for divorce if she is denied her *onah*.[13]

So important is the conjugal act that rabbis codified in Jewish law how frequently men of various occupations should perform their husbandly duty. Laborers working out of town and merchants who travel to buy and sell should perform it once a week; laborers working in the town where they live, twice weekly. Men of strong constitution, tax-exempt and enjoying a profitable home business, are commanded to nightly duty.[14] Not much room for the proverbial "headache" in this order.

Hebrew commentators in the last hundred years have agreed that unusual medical problems are the only grounds for practicing birth control, Eisenstein wrote. Even abstinence—which appears to be a "natural" and passive form of birth control—is out of the question because it violates the law of the husband to provide *onah*. Furthermore, it would violate the Genesis 1:28 mandate to be fruitful, which also falls on the husband.[15]

> We see from all this that Orthodox Jewish law places a very positive emphasis on large families. Large families are regarded as unmitigated blessings....The commentary expresses this in its customary figure of speech, by asserting that in Messianic days, women will give birth every day.[16]

Why the Hebrew Family Model?

That a daily trip to the delivery room stirs anything but thoughts of paradise on earth shows that something has been lost over the ages. Human fertility, and all that it means, no longer is the prized possession it once was to our Jewish forefathers.

But is there any point in Christians' dwelling upon the values of the Hebrew culture? Does the New Covenant obliterate all that came before it?

Romans 3:1-2 says the Jews have advantages—first, "that they were entrusted with the oracles of God." The church was grafted in to these same people, says Romans 11, comparing them to the rich root of a cultivated olive tree. Christians must not be arrogant toward the root, but must "remember that it is not you who supports the root, but the root supports you" (11:18).

Hebrews 8:6 says we are heirs of a better covenant than the old one. Yet we are not to despise the Old Testament. Three times (Heb. 10:16; 8:10; 2 Cor. 3:3) the New Testament echoes the Jeremiah 31:33 prophecy that God will make a new covenant with Israel in which "I will put My law within them, and on their heart will I write it." While the New Testament lifts the burden of strict adherence to the sometimes tedious requirements of the Law, the spirit of the Law remains. A careful look at the Old Testament cannot help but conclude that God's initial command to man—to be fruitful and multiply—pervades the history of His chosen people. We will see in a later chapter that the New Testament generally reaffirms this intention.

This spirit of multiplication toward fulfilling the growing reign of God on earth is an integral part of our legacy from the patriarchs. To deny this is to deny the very life-giving nature of our Father God as revealed in His Word and manifested in the natural, uninhibited functioning of a united man and woman, made in God's divine image.

Jesus said He came not to abolish the Law, but to *fulfill* it, and that "not the smallest letter or stroke shall pass away from the Law, until all is accomplished" (Matt. 5:18). The earth's population may exceed five billion people, but not all is accomplished. There is still land to be subdued. There remains evil to be vanquished. There are souls to be won for Christ. Christian couples should treasure their Old Testament heritage that orders intercourse toward fertility and that prizes fertility for the perpetuation of family name and blessing. God wants the spirit of every aspect of His Law to be engraved not on tablets of stone, but on our hearts.

PART 3

THE CHOICE

The Choice

FIVE

BIRTH CONTROL: RIGHT OR WRONG?

> *Where the Spirit of the Lord is, there is liberty.*
>
> (2 Corinthians 3:17).

When his lover popped the pill, the late Richard Brautigan wrote in his poem "The Pill Versus the Springhill Mining Disaster," that he couldn't help but think of all the people lost inside.

At least he had the thought. It's one that never even occurs to most consumers of contraceptives. And that includes Christians, who diligently don condoms by night and by day gush pro-family rhetoric, fight abortion, bad-mouth free birth control handouts, build schools in every church basement, and who, for the most part in America, enjoy the highest standard of living anyone could ever hope for. It seems that we're keen on kids. So how come we don't give more thought to all those potential lives lost inside?

The very concept of *planning* a family, of scheduling the arrival of children as if they were out-of-town guests to be shoehorned into a busy summer schedule, hits at the heart of the blessing-or-burden dilemma. If conception is a blessing, is it right to try to limit it? Or avoid it altogether? Is artificial birth control wrong, as the Roman Catholic church says? And if there is some element of spiritual transgression, what about the tough cases: the impoverished family already saddled with children it can't care for, the unstable couple close to divorce, the home racked by alcoholism? Or for that matter, what about the happy, stable couple that says "thanks, but no thanks, we'd rather stay childless?"

Scripture says little directly about birth control. But it does offer this: some key principles by which couples can approach the matter and find God's will for themselves. To better understand the matter, let's trace Biblical and church thought on birth control. We'll also look at the secular birth control/population lobby of the last two centuries that has given us the modern luxury of effective contraception.

What Was Onan's Sin?

Shortly before our marriage, my wife and I discussed contraception matter-of-factly. It was like our checkbook or our two Volkswagens—another tool by which we'd manage our family. And the tools were fairly reliable. Effectiveness approaches one hundred percent for the most popular forms of birth control used properly. We would have no whines before their time.

This sophisticated ability to limit conception with artificial devices, and with almost guaranteed success, is relatively new. The desire to do so is not.

Imagine, on some enchanted evening by the Nile, pulling out some pulverized crocodile dung in fermented mucilage (a gooey plant substance). This was one of several contraceptive formulas found on Egyptian papyri dating from 1900 to 1100 B.C., wrote John T. Noonan Jr. in his comprehensive book, *Contraception.* Dozens of other potions and practices, most with dubious effectiveness (the Greek Soranos recommended that a woman hold her breath, rise, squat, sneeze, and wash), have been used through the ages.[1]

One of the oldest, most common and still current (though not very effective) methods of birth control also happens to be the practice used in the Bible's one explicit—and highly controversial—passage on the subject. That was Onan's use of *coitus interruptus*, or withdrawal (Gen. 38). This is where semination takes place outside the vagina after intercourse. Following Onan's withdrawal during intercourse with Tamar, God took his life.

Unfortunately, the certainty of this passage's moral does not match the finality of its outcome for Onan. He was not merely frustrating a conception; he was also violating the levirate marriage law, under which he was bound to raise up children to carry on the name of his deceased brother, Er, Tamar's first husband.

You've heard of reading between the lines? The cause for Onan's punishment has been debated and over analyzed in the Talmud and other Jewish writings to the point of attributing Er's demise to some similar procreative sin. Genesis, though, has no greater indictment of Er other than to say he was "evil." Most Jewish scholars feel that while an "intimation" of evil regarding birth control can be drawn from Onan's act, no sweeping ban of contraception can be determined from this one instance alone.[2] Noonan likewise concluded "that contraception is not the act for which Onan was killed."[3]

Noonan's modern view, however, has not been the dominant one through church history. The first main application of the Onan passage was to counter the fourth-century Gnostics, who opposed procreation and, in some cases, marriage.[4] Augustine, Calvin, and many other church writers through the centuries have argued against contraception on the basis of Onan's sin. Protestants have generally offered less rigorous interpretations. In recent decades, with widespread approval of birth control (outside of Catholic orthodoxy), Onan is rarely mentioned.

For the Hebrews, contraception was almost a moot point because of the commandments to marry and to procreate. The infant church reaffirmed the propriety of marriage and procreation, but diluted their glory by exalting virginity as well. Some historians consider that what emerged as the Christian consensus on marriage and procreation was a compromise. On one side was the deep pro-natalist Jewish root. The other was the general thrust of some of the popular earticklers of the day who tended to oppose sex (and therefore procreation, in some cases) as fleshly indulgences: Gnostics, Dualists (who espoused two eternal and opposing principles or beings, one good and the other evil), and strict Ascetics (who renounced comfort and social life for solitude and religious devotion).

As a result, Noonan writes, most early church fathers felt that "virginity is preferred, but intercourse in marriage, for procreation only, is permissible."[5] The Scriptural basis was 1 Corinthians 7, Paul's most extensive passage on sex and the worthiness of virginity.

This is not to say that virginity was suddenly enshrined. On balance were passages in 1 Timothy that affirmed the good of procreation: "Women shall be preserved through the bearing of children" (2:15) and "Therefore, I want younger widows to get married, bear children..." (5:14). In other epistles, marriage is spoken of highly.

Augustine's writings are considered the most influential for shaping general church thought on procreation and marriage. Through most of church history, procreation was "regarded as the primary purpose of marriage and a major justification for sexual intercourse."[6] The Catholic church has continued to forbid artificial birth control (as opposed to rhythmic abstinence), though its more recent pronouncements have acknowledged the importance of sex for conjugal unity (as opposed to sex for procreation only) within marriage. The long-standing emphasis on sex for procreation shifted toward sex for unity, or companionship, during the Reformation, and the trend has accelerated in our age.

"Compatibility," for example, is considered by many as the only worthy grounds for marital stability, be it sexual compatibility or otherwise. The nebulous idea of "incompatibility," by the same token, is grounds for easy divorce. The old argument of "staying together for the sake of the children" has all but disappeared. In its place we have the psychobabble of the 1970s and 1980s that emphasizes the adults and treats *them* as children—emotionally retarded children, that is, who need "space to grow" or who are somehow "maturing" past the level of their partners.

By contrast, have you ever heard of a man seeking divorce because his wife was barren? Under some older interpretations of Jewish law, as we have seen, barrenness after ten years was grounds for divorce. This, of course, violates the Christian view of covenantal marriage, and later Jewish scholars came to feel the same way. But the premise of the earlier position again shows that we've come a long, long way in the priority we place on procreation and the appraisal of children as blessings.

This Message Brought to You by...

The historical foundations regarding birth control, therefore, were largely religious and prohibitive. Onan's example was so well-known, and so widely interpreted as *prima facie* evidence against contraception, that the term *onanism* came into the language. It referred to the sin of *coitus interruptus*, or masturbation, or incomplete coitus in general.

It was against these pillars of centuries-old, religiously based disapproval that the modern birth control movement began to chip away. It wasn't easy. But in the end, the pillars crumbled. To fully understand the impact of this change on the Biblical view of fertility, it is critical to examine some of the determined rebels who fought for change, what their underlying philosophies were, and what their self-righteous pleas have led to.

Though birth control has existed in some form for virtually all of recorded history, the modern birth control movement originated in eighteenth-century Europe. Its leading spokesman was English clergyman and economist Thomas Robert Malthus (1766-1834). From his name we get the adjective *Malthusian*, which refers to the still-popular theory that population tends to outrun its means of food supply, and that if it goes unchecked, poverty and misery will result.

Even with his fears of population growth, Malthus rejected contraception as immoral. It mattered little. Subsequent French and English writers, called neo-Malthusians, had no problem with espousing contraception. The condom was already in use, made first from animal membranes, and after the vulcanization of rubber (1843-44), it was made from that more reliable substance. The birth control issue stayed hot in Europe, and a fertility decline became evident in Western Europe by 1875.

There is evidence that abortion and *coitus interruptus* were also significant factors in the reduced birth rate during this era.[7] While a significant number of couples may have practiced withdrawal during the mid-nineteenth century in England, others used more drastic abortive measures: sticking a knitting needle into the uterus, or ingesting substances in quantities large enough to threaten the mother's life.[8] Withdrawal is still practiced, in widely varying degrees, in other societies today.

In America, the birth control movement got on the front burner around the turn of the century. Its evolution falls into distinct ideological phases, according to an analysis by familiographer Allan Carlson in his newsletter from the Rockford Institute Center on the Family in America.[9]

The First Radical Phase (1900-1920)

The women's movement was already stirring in the late 1800s. Concerns over it, along with free love, easy divorce, contraceptive use by the upper classes, and over breeding by the lower classes, resulted in a "race suicide" scare. Even President Theodore Roosevelt tackled the issue, referring to

> Americans who avoided having children as "criminals against the race...the object of contemptuous abhorrence by healthy people." Addressing the National Congress of Mothers in 1905, Roosevelt condemned the "viciousness, coldness, shallow-heartedness" of women who refused to do "their duty," especially the growing number of college-educated women, over half of whom remained unmarried. Birth control, he said, was sinful and denied to the nation the necessary growing population and stock of large, stable families.[10]

Opposition such as this from the highest levels rankled some American feminists. The more activist women imported liberal sexual attitudes from Europe, condemned men and formed socialist and anti-capitalist alliances. The International Workers of the World included sexual radicalism and anti-natalism in their program, declaring in 1915

> "that 'a woman has the right to control her own body,' that 'unfit children ought not to be born into the world,' that 'scientific knowledge of sex-physiology can never be classified as impure or obscene,' and that the masses 'have no right to add sufferers to the already too many competing for bread.'"[11]

Sound familiar? These demands of the violence-prone IWW were shocking at the time. Now they are the frequently spoken—and widely accepted—arguments of abortionists, feminists, arrogant population planners, and the most liberal sex education advocates. It was by no means the last time that yesterday's radical ideology would become tomorrow's gospel.

This battlefield between tradition and progressivism was the training ground for Margaret Sanger, the mother of the American birth control movement, including what was to become Planned Parenthood. She was a labor organizer for IWW, then turned to the contraception issue in 1913, "a move reinforced by several trips to Europe and a love affair with English sexologist Havelock Ellis."[12] Her English lover was hardly one to remind her of the divine link between sex and procreation. He was a leading sexual revolutionary, as well as "an extreme fetishist (a devotee of 'golden showers,' or urination), impotent with his lesbian wife, and a sufferer from premature ejaculation."[13]

Margaret Sanger, more committed to promoting herself than the fashionable socialism of her day, became involved with birth control "almost by default," writes feminist Germaine Greer.[14] One of Ms. Sanger's early public splashes came in 1916. She broke state law and netted valuable newspaper coverage by establishing a birth control clinic in Brooklyn, New York, which was closed by police nine days after it opened. Ms. Greer suggests that repeated grandstanding by Ms. Sanger and fellow birth control advocate Marie Stopes actually did little to enhance the ability of individuals to control their reproduction. Rather, they set in motion changes that were to further undermine traditional family authority in later decades: "What they did do was create the precedent for the invasion of privacy which made reproductive behavior a public matter and placed its regulation in the hands of the medical and pharmaceutical establishment."[15]

By 1920, the birth control movement was no longer considered so radical. The U.S. government, fearful of venereal disease, began to issue condoms to soldiers and sailors; condom sales began to rise; Madison Avenue adopted sex in its promotions.[16]

The Eugenics Phase (1920-1940)

The "race suicide" adherents saw by 1920 that the birth control movement was getting out of hand. The affluent classes were coming to like contraception, regardless of the effect on the nation's overall fertility and so-called purity of stock. In the interest of eugenics (the improvement of a race's hereditary qualities), there was only one logical step. If the elite refused to outbreed the commoners, then the upper class would have to bring contraception to the masses. Margaret Sanger was ready. She abandoned her radicalism and cultivated the more palatable cause of saving an unenlightened world. She saw the task this way: "a battle of a republic against the machinations of the Roman Catholic church."[17] She had touched a public nerve:

> Hostile to mass society and believing, with atheist Robert Ingersoll, that "ignorance, poverty, and vice are populating the world," the eugenicists flocked to the birth control cause, joining with Sanger in 1922 to create the Birth Control Federation of America (BCFA).[18]

Though her apologists stress that eugenics was not her prime motivation, it's clear Ms. Sanger welcomed the newly fashionable eugenic ideas of the age. She wrote in 1926 that the insane and feeble-minded should be sterilized; in 1939, that she and her followers had sought to limit procreation of the "unfit," while other eugenicists had fought to increase multiplication of the "rich."[19] She felt the poor had large families only because of ignorance; given the proper information and tools, they would naturally limit their families. This has proven to be false, in the United States and around the world (see chapter 9). She complained that European immigrants "were ignorant of hygiene, made the cities wretched, and threatened to replace native workers."[20]

Another group Ms. Sanger helped found was the Population Association of America. Its first president, Henry Pratt Fairchild, was the leading academic racist of the interwar period.[21] And he was hardly the last of the breed. Ultra-right and libertarian racists continue to be among the biggest proponents of population controls today, issuing alarmist tracts about immigration, racial purity and "native stock." Ms. Sanger and colleague Marie Stopes were also of this same mold—"radicals of the extreme right" by Germaine Greer's analysis—and therefore a stumbling block to the allegedly noble democratic ideas of that era's feminism.[22]

Ms. Stopes's obsession with refining and preserving a superior breed would have qualified her for a chief propagandist position in Hitler's regime. In a 1919 article, "Mrs. Jones Does Her Worst," she questioned of Mrs. Jones's children: "Are these puny-faced, ill-balanced, feeble, ungainly, withered children the young of an imperial race?" Mrs. Jones's unqualified breeding, Marie Stopes judged, was "destroying the race." Ms. Stopes once castigated in writing the superintendent of a school for the deaf for allowing a deaf couple to have children, who were also deaf.[23] When Ms. Stopes's son failed to let Mom choose his bride, as she had wished, and married a woman who wore spectacles, Marie Stopes refused to recognize her daughter-in-law.[24]

Children are not unqualified blessings under the restrictive economy of eugenics. Only those who serve to further *humanity's* best interests are counted as blessed; no life is automatically sacred because it is made in the image of God. This is a clear expression of what our era has come to label secular humanism—a man-centered, God-rejecting value system.

In the fertile eugenicist climate of the 1920s and 1930s, Birth Control Federation of America clinics began to spread. Catholic officials failed in a legal challenge to the federation in 1929 and thereby enhanced the image of the clinics. As the clinics spread, the eugenicists became disillusioned. It was clear that poor folks didn't give a hoot about narrowing their families. Failing to grasp the new, progressive thought, the lower classes continued in their common sense to regard their children as blessings. Consequently, the overall effect of birth control was "dysgenic," that is, discouraging the "best stock" from reproducing. It was time for some new marketing.

Pro-Family Phase (1940-1960)

Sure enough, a public relations counselor came up with the goods—a name change. The stodgy-sounding Birth Control Federation of America changed its moniker to Planned Parenthood Federation of America.

It was a well-calculated step. The movement effected a pro-family slant, a marked shift from its radical, tainted past. In this new homogenized form, not the woman but the entire family became the focus

> of reproductive control. Social peace and harmony, resting on contented families, became the birth control goal. The PPFA program saw mutual sexual enjoyment as the new cement

of modern marriage, the source for renewed family stability after the turmoil of earlier decades. Women's sexual repression was the problem to be overcome, albeit only within the confines of the family. Talk of "women's rights" vanished from PPFA literature. The organization's literature presented very traditional male and female roles. Aid and advice was restricted to married women, as PPFA assumed a norm of premarital chastity and turned the unmarried away. Abortion was considered to be a form of murder.[25]

Planning! That was the key. Better use of family and global resources, an improved standard of living—such were the goals to be sought through efficient control over conceptions. Rational planning for such noble ideals replaced the outdated and disproven "good stock" ideas of eugenics. There was a new respectability to the idea of birth control, or more properly, family planning. Yet the movement was still relegated to the private domain. There was no government money or propaganda involved, no challenge to anti-birth control laws on the books (though rarely enforced) at state and federal levels.[26]

Re-Radicalization Phase (1960-Current)

This relatively modest stance did not last long. The overpopulation scare began in the 1950s and culminated with the publication of Paul Ehrlich's apocalyptic book *The Population Bomb*. This was Malthusian scare propaganda, twentieth-century style, and it had several consequences for the birth control movement. It also helps explain why Planned Parenthood did not remain the meek family support group it purported to be.

> First, Planned Parenthood quietly shed the pro-family label, as the population crisis let childless adults off the hook. To refuse to marry or to bear children were no longer anti-social acts. Indeed, in an "overpopulated" world, avoiding children had become a positive expression of social responsibility. Second, the "crisis" environment seemed to justify drastic actions. Unmarried women could no longer be denied (birth control) services. Sexually active teenagers also became an important new category of clients. Abortion was recast as a necessary option for an overpopulated world. Third, the "population crisis" coincided with rapid expansion of "entitlements" at the federal level, and birth control became another "service" to be provided by the growing American welfare state.[27]

As if the overpopulation myth wasn't enough voltage for the birth control movement, along came a rejuvenated feminist movement to make sure the status quo toppled. The cleverly phrased "women's right to control our bodies," which abortionists continue to allege, came forth as rationale for better and more available contraceptives. It furthermore was grounds for the related demands of better sex education and health care, and elimination of laws that interfered with the new sexual freedoms.

In the midst of this clamor, the public/private distinction collapsed. Congress, in 1970, passed an act to get contraception to low-income women. The 1972 Report of the President's Commission on Population Growth and the American Future actually *denounced families with more than two children* and recommended providing contraceptives to teenagers. In 1973, the Supreme Court legalized abortion, and before long federal dollars were helping to subsidize this national genocide. Demand for population controls grew through the 1970s, and other federal aid for family planning services was approved. "By 1980, the federal government could claim a comprehensive national fertility-control program."[28]

We had come a long way from Teddy Roosevelt's rebuke about not having enough babies.

It is no accident that the final cultural grafting of birth control has coincided with the rise of divorce, as well as the virtual extinction of sexual mores—any age, any partner, any method is OK. God did not intend for procreation to be the sole purpose of marriage and sex. But to remove procreation altogether from the sex act—an option now refined by modern birth control—dilutes responsibility, whether in a moral or paternal sense, in the sex act. It makes it easier for sex to become nothing more than a great American pastime.

Sex, of course, should be fun. Outside of its procreative side, it offers a rich depth to a couple's pleasure and bonding. And couples who are infertile, because of age or physiological problems, must be content with the companionship element of sex.

The problem is that, when society trivializes the procreative element from marital sex in favor of the companionship element, it becomes difficult to draw the line against sex outside of marriage. In liberal parlance, it would be discriminatory to bar unmarrieds from their "right" to have sex. Once purely recreational sex is tolerated outside of marriage, who is to judge against any practice that leads to orgasmic release—masturbation, homosexuality, bestiality and other perversions?

Birth control and de-emphasized procreation pose a further problem in that they sabotage the traditional Christian norm of marriage as a lifelong, covenant institution. "Staying together for the sake of the kids" may seem cruel for the disenchanted partners. It may mean a less-than-healthy environment for child raising. But if the presence of children becomes an incentive to seek marital counseling, an adhesive for a pairing that Scripture says is holy and lifelong, it is good. Who knows how many of the millions of divorces taking place occur too rashly because there are no children to temper the decision?

Contra-contraception

Rising divorce, vanishing sexual taboos, and a full-fledged, state-sponsored fertility control program are among the sad hallmarks of the latter half of the twentieth century. If the trends continue, the family will disintegrate further, unraveling the entire social fabric with it. Birth control is not the sole culprit here. But its widespread acceptance and availability have greased the skids on this downward moral spiral.

And Christians share the blame.

A religious populace that would have scorned such cavalier use of contraception a century ago now considers family planning an inalienable right. With the exception of Catholic moral teaching (as opposed to its application by the laity) there has been in recent decades no major Christian opposition—by formal declaration or popular example—to hard-core contraceptive addiction. A few denominations even tolerate abortion, buying into the Nazi-like logic of Margaret Sanger and others that the unfit life is better not lived. The Religious Coalition for Abortion Rights in 1987 listed thirty-two members, whose organizational names suggest some ties with Jews and most mainline Christian denominations.

The Catholic church has continually opposed artificial birth control and therefore has been at odds with the modern obsession for recreational sex. Much to its credit, it has done so on the grounds of the divine link between procreation and marriage. God bless Pope John Paul II and the popes before him for maintaining a prophetic stance and then standing firm. Unfortunately, there are few fertile couples willing to taste this salty word.

After all, a young working couple's spontaneous nights out at tony restaurants, their carefree consumer acquisitions, their annual ski weekends, not to mention the wife's career, would become endangered species if babies kept sprouting every other year. Companionship and climaxes rate higher than procreation on the list of most young Americans.

And there's no reason to think American Catholics are too much different from their neighbors. A 1987

Time magazine poll found that only twenty-four percent of American Catholics believe artificial birth control is wrong. And you can't help but wonder how many of the respondents in that twenty-four percent are struggling young couples with fertile wives.[29]

John Paul may be the most influential Christian of our age to renounce birth control, but he is not the only one. Christian seminar leader Bill Gothard is another.

Gothard not only rejects birth control but embraces the Hebrew heritage of a two-week abstinence from intercourse (see chapter 3). He cites Leviticus 15:19-20 for abstaining during the week of menstrual uncleanness and Leviticus 15:28 for abstaining during the second week, in which the cleansing is completed. Gothard's *Advanced Seminar Textbook* includes testimonies from couples practicing the two-week abstinence who have experienced better sex lives, more meaningful marriages, and, since the two weeks end at the peak of ovulation, easier conceptions. He also presents a doctor's statement that the two-week abstinence may decrease the incidence of certain infections and genetic abnormalities.[30] Other medical problems associated with the use of certain contraceptives, notably pills and some intrauterine devices, have been widely documented.

Then there is the outspoken author Mary Pride, an ex-feminist who is now a Christian. In *The Way Home*, a vigorous Biblical argument for "homeworking" mothers instead of mothers working outside the home, she takes the traditional view of Onan's sin as proving the sinfulness of contraception. She considers "deliberate marital barrenness" to be "perverted" sex and ranks it with "masturbation, homosexuality, lesbianism, bestiality, prostitution, adultery."[31]

A Big Chip on the Shoulder

There exists, therefore, an impressive church tradition, an alarming secular legacy, some Scriptures and some common-sense factors that pose serious questions against birth control. Some Christians see the bottom line in all this as complete contraceptive abstinence for the duration of a marriage. The trouble is that to formulate a doctrine that birth control is always sinful is to step slightly beyond the Bible. It means indulgence in legalism and perfectionism.

Have you fed the hungry lately? Have you taken in strangers? Have you visited prisoners? If you have not done all three, you have arguably violated Matthew 25:35-36. Have you visited orphans? Widows? Look at James 1:27 and then check your spiritual oil.

Far be it from me to say you're sinning if you've never done these things, or if you haven't done them with sufficient frequency. The point is that a perfectionist approach to Scripture, even to the New Testament, can yield one a vacation at the nearest asylum. To interpret the Onan story or the 1 Timothy passage (that women shall be saved by childbearing) as absolute prohibitions against contraception is to stretch them to a point of perfection that is not evident to most readers. And as for Mosaic law passages, such as the menstrual cleanness sections of Leviticus, it is legalism for Christians to feel compelled to obey these.

To have God instill in you a conviction, especially when shared by a spouse, to refrain from birth control, can be a wonderful thing, well-grounded in Scripture. To impose a personal conviction on the shoulders of those not able to bear it (especially your spouse!) is to be like a religious lawyer weighing people down with burdens too difficult to bear. Jesus condemned that.

Christians are under a new jurisdiction with its own new code, though it may have several similarities with the 613 laws of the old code, argues Arnold Fruchtenbaum in *Hebrew Christianity*. Those who dabble in keeping Mosaic laws, he warns, must not assume others are required to follow in their path. "This is equally wrong and borders on legalism. The one who exercises his freedom to keep the Law must recognize and respect another's freedom not to keep it."[32]

Mention freedom, and some Christians are ready to jettison portions of Scripture and godly discipline. After all, "where the Spirit of the Lord is, there is liberty." Yet the "freedom" to interfere with conception, to violate the spirit of the Genesis 1:28 mandate to populate the earth abundantly, is not grounded in the Bible. It is, rather, a hard-fought license earned by a collection of feminists, atheists, racists, utopians and sexual revolutionaries. A gift from a coalition such as this should be automatically suspect.

The agenda of the birth control movement is now out in the open. It regards children as a burden and Genesis 1:28 as asinine. It is, therefore, diametrically opposed to God's view.

It would be a serious overreaction, under the guise of New Testament freedom, to dissociate family planning from Scripture or Spirit-led direction. Wanting to bear children is not just an arbitrary predisposition, such as liking fried onion rings. For example, as much as I was in love with my wife and looked forward to marriage, I did not sense an innate knack for coping with diaper pins and 3:00 a.m. screams. I had no visions of being father of a multitude. I had no qualms about using contraception; I did not fret over the quiet mining disaster going on inside my wife.

But through the Bible, the Holy Spirit's leading, and the example of other families, God unfolded to me a bit of His perspective on fertility. Along the way, two elements have broadened my ability to cope with the responsibility of entering into parenthood with four sons: faith and obedience.

In addition to the foundational Scripture that has already been presented, I believe faith and obedience are keys to the whole dilemma of blessing that masquerades as burden. In the next chapter, we'll see how these keys can help open up a couple's deliberations over having children and how they can help unlock the mystery of successfully reckoning children as blessings.

Six

Birth Control:
Building a Better
Incubator

> *And without faith it is impossible to*
> *please Him, for he who comes to God*
> *must believe that He is, and that He is*
> *a rewarder of those who seek Him.*
>
> Hebrews 11:6

Remember Ananias and Sapphira?

This couple made a brief but memorable appearance in Acts 5. They were blessed with property. They were told by the Holy Spirit to sell it and give the proceeds to the church. Instead, the couple violated that prompting and withheld some of the funds.

They may have thought they were savvy traders—trying to get the best from both God and man—but they were not prepared for Peter. He was acting upon inside information, courtesy of the Holy Spirit. When Peter confronted Ananias and Sapphira with their hidden action, they dropped dead. Their blessing of property had become their curse.

Property and wealth afflict many in our day as well. It's hard to find middle-class Americans who don't have at least one credit card. Plastic money, as it's called, is a luxury-blessing—it frees the user from carrying large amounts of cash or writing excessive numbers of checks. Yet thousands of otherwise intelligent people, many with high incomes, bring their families to virtual financial ruin by abusing credit. The burden of debt eroding the blessing of assets is too often the result.

To bring the analogy closer to the issue of children as blessings or burdens, how about marriage? One need only think of the pain of divorce, the lasting hurts, the traumas for the children, the wasted years, and for women over forty, the likelihood of a gloomy, lonely future. Finding a spouse is the greatest imaginable longing for many young adults, and the greatest blessing when it happens. Yet many a divorced man or woman would just as adamantly say that their marriage was life's cruelest jest.

Marriage, real estate profits, and credit cards—these are obviously blessings for many people, though their reckoning as plus or minus is not a matter of luck or fate. Handled properly, they benefit the holder. They can just as easily become like a curse.

God also sends intended blessings our way in the form of children. But make no mistake: Children, like so many apparently good things, can also be a burden. *Whether an intended blessing becomes a curse depends on the attitude and stewardship of the recipient.*

A Christian couple I know has four children. Mom is happy to stay home with the children. Dad struggles hard as a self- employed contractor. The family has some debts, but they are being reduced. Unlike most of their home-owning friends, they still rent their home, but they are content. They are committed church members and have ordered their lives to mature continually in Christ. This couple has a Scripturally based conviction to refrain from birth control. To top it off, Mom has a good fifteen or more fertile years ahead—enough to at least *triple* their four little ones.

"Every time we've had a baby, God has increased my salary," Dad says. He believes that God will continue to provide the needed money.

This couple, then, is walking in faith and obedience. Were they not, they would find it difficult to count their children, or the family's general circumstances, as blessings. Let's examine more closely the role faith and obedience play in having a positive outlook on a growing family.

Impossible Without Faith

"And without faith, *it is impossible* to please Him" (Heb. 11:6, italics added). It's no accident that family planning was pioneered by humanists, some of them atheists, whose faith lay not in the divine. The humanist always wants to direct his own destiny; the more control the better, because he sees history as a random happening apart from divine intervention.

Many of today's Christians, unfortunately, have a humanistic approach to destiny. Even when a committed Christian couple takes up the matter of family planning, it's easy to forget to ask God to take the third seat on the planning board of directors. This is asking for trouble. Christ demands *complete* lordship over our lives.

Let's be honest. It's not a rational act to submit fully your most intimate decisions to a Spirit-being you've never seen and to the intents and commands of His law book. It is an act of faith. The Bible says anyone who forsakes the appearance of things and trusts in God based on a "conviction of things not seen" (Heb. 11:1) is exercising faith. God reckons such a person as righteous.

The practice of faith has a direct application on family planning, though it does not have to be an all-or-nothing proposition. Some parents feel they've reached their limit of children with one child. Others may feel their quiver holds only three. Some may have a dozen before their cup runneth over.

But other parents may feel they've reached their limit and then, with God's leading, willingly refrain from using contraception. They are stepping out in faith if they believe God will order their attitudes and circumstances in ways "not seen" at present to make any further children welcome as blessings.

Their willingness to risk sacrificing a comfortable family size is (roughly speaking) proportional to their faith in this area. After all, "God has allotted to each *a measure* of faith" (Rom. 12:3, italics added). No condemnation needs to be heaped on one whose faith doesn't measure up to another's. Romans 14:22 says, "The faith which you have, have as your own conviction before God."

Periodic use of birth control does not necessarily mean a couple is failing to exercise faith in family planning. Ideally, both partners continually keep the matter open before God. The prayerful consideration should not be over when to *stop* using birth control, as if that were the equivalent of quitting your job and going out to evangelize Africa (though moving to Africa may seem more palatable than keeping the home and filling it with more of your own young heathens). Rather, sexual relations open to conception should be seen as *normal*. Prayer and counsel should seek God's approval to do something different.

So how else does faith apply? It may be faith that God will provide money for obstetric care and delivery. It may be faith that morning sickness will not be so bad, or that God will supernaturally help Mom to endure it. It may be faith that God will provide a larger house when the new baby arrives. It may be faith that God will give Mom and Dad the patience, energy, time, and so forth to labor with still one more child for eighteen or more years. Note the second half of Hebrews 11:6: "And without faith it is impossible to please Him, for he who comes to God must believe that He is, and that *He is a rewarder of those who seek Him*" (italics added). There's nothing faithless about "looking to the reward" (Heb. 11:26) and hoping to get a taste of it while on earth.

And there is a longer-range faith that looks to a more distant reward. You could call it radical vision. It says, "I don't care about the money and inconvenience and sacrifice of having children because I believe God has marked my children to win souls and wreak havoc against the kingdom of darkness, and I believe He's equipped me to train them for it, and as long as my spouse and I are capable of matching egg with sperm we'll remain open to God's gift of conception. If my reward doesn't become manifest on earth, I know it's safely stored up in heaven."

I cannot boast that I have that measure of faith, and I hope this book will inflict no condemnation on sincere Christians who find themselves in the same boat. My hope is that couples of child-bearing age will simply be open to the possibility of a family larger than what they may have planned on their own.

That marginal child, that fruit of faith, could turn out to be a Billy Graham. Or a president of the United States. Or, more simply, it may be the one child who refrains from moving out of town as an adult and is there to care for you in old age.

You think you've met your quota of having two children? Or gone above and beyond the call of duty by having four? You may very well have, but don't jump to any conclusions.

Consider the Wesley family. Susanna Wesley was the *twenty-fifth* child of her parents, notes Bill Gothard in his Christian seminar materials. Had she herself stopped with even a dozen deliveries, the world would have never known John Wesley or Charles Wesley. John was her fifteenth child; Charles was her eighteenth (though only ten of nineteen survived infancy). John was a leader of the Great Awakening in England and America and founded the Methodist movement. Charles was a Methodist leader and wrote six thousand hymns, many of them still sung today.[1]

Gothard also notes the influence of Jonathan Edwards, the only son among eleven children and the leader of the Great Awakening in America. His descendants included three college presidents, sixty-five college professors, one hundred lawyers, thirty judges, sixty-six medical doctors and eight holders of public office, including three senators, three governors and one United States vice president.[2] Only God knows the marvelous plans— some mighty, some sublime—He has on the boards for every life that issues from the womb.

The bottom line on faith is that you can't please God without it. Romans 14:23 says it even stronger: "Whatever is not from faith is sin." Family planning without your own measure of faith mixed in displeases God.

The Fruits of Obedience

As Hebrews 11:6 points out, God's reward for faith falls to those who seek Him. Those seeking God are studying His Word, communing in prayer, walking in fellowship with believers, submitting to the counsel of wise brethren. They are working out their overall faith by employing obedience to God's ways.

Obedience, of course, is part of the normal Christian walk regardless of the opportunity for procreation. But in the realm of family, obedience to God's Word can make the difference in whether children become a blessing or a burden to a family.

The fruit of blessings and prosperity falling upon those who obey God is a constant thread through the Bible, especially the Old Testament. Deuteronomy 28, the blessing-and-curse chapter examined earlier, provides numerous graphic illustrations of the blessings of obedience, including wealth and fertility. It

lists poverty and infertility among the curses of disobedience.

The book of Proverbs outlines all sorts of good tid-
ings that will come to the righteous ones who purpose
to obey Biblical injunctions regarding diligence, pru-
dence, truth, wisdom, and generosity. The man obedient to the principle of tithing, for example, finds his
barns filled with plenty and his vats overflowing with
new wine (Prov. 3:10).

Or look at it this way. You don't have to earn an
M.B.A, look after Number One, claw your way to the
top, cheat the IRS, or invest in a bull stock market to
become prosperous. In fact, trusting only in those
strategies will head you in the opposite direction—if
not in this world then certainly in the next, Scripture
promises. The blessings of success, contentment,
wealth, and prestige tend to fall to covenant-keepers.
The disobedient get the curses.

So what does this have to do with having a large
family? Children are more apparently a blessing in a
godly, ordered, happy, financially secure home than
in one that lacks those qualities. By the same token,
children tend to be a burden in a home that lacks
godly discipline, self-sacrifice, two loving parents,
and adequate material provision.

Imagine two parents who pay no greater heed to
Christianity than to daydream in front of a preacher
once a week. Dad travels a lot during the week.
When he's home week nights, he prefers watching
television rather than attending to the needs of his
one child, a seven-year-old girl. He's gone most
weekends, hunting or fishing with friends who share
his interest in draining six-packs of beer.

Mom resents all of the above. Consequently, communication, sex, and overall fellowship with her husband of eleven years are at an all-time low. But she puts all that behind her when she escapes to her sales job at the department store. And she doesn't feel so guilty about the job now that her daughter has entered first grade; after all, day care is only a few hours a day now. To compensate for the overall dreariness of her life, she has taken to shopping sprees with charge cards and extended the family's debt in the process. She's a working woman now, she tells herself, and she has to dress well, especially for the new male sales manager, who seems to enjoy her jokes so much when they share a sandwich after hours.

With both parents storing up their treasure in unheavenly corners, there is no one left to minister to the emotional problems beginning to be manifest in their daughter. Her teacher tries to explain some things to Mom and Dad, but they both shrug it off. "She'll grow out of it," Dad says.

Obedience to God's principles is seriously lacking in this household. Faith in His miraculous ability to effect change does not even enter the minds of this worldly pair.

No outsider could judge whether this ordinary family should or should not expand. But should God allow them another conception, the intended blessing might well be twisted into a burden. If you envision the sum of a family's relationships as a balancing scale, an additional child here could intensify the existing strain. Yet ideally, each child should somehow bring a new equilibrium to any family's balance.

That's not to say a child that strains a family could never emerge as an emotionally balanced adult, a self-sufficient worker, and a mature Christian. After all, to rule out children strictly on the basis of their odds for success is to parrot the flimsy logic of the abortion rights advocate. But the point in the example is: There's no use kidding this Mr. and Mrs. that the next baby is going to be an unmitigated blessing from God. In their skewed cosmos of self-interest and modern idolatry, another so-called blessing of a child just doesn't compute on their books.

Let's return to the couple I know who has, in faith, rejected birth control and has had four visits from the stork. Their standard of living is lower than the working couple just examined. But to cite just one difference in the realm of obedience, the growing family adheres to the godly quality of contentment. They have every worldly reason to be discontent with their rental home, in a not-so-nice part of town, lacking air conditioning during the steamy Alabama summers. But they have chosen to obey 1 Timothy 6:8, which commands contentment with the bare necessities. Even living in the same home with double the number of children, they would still enjoy a higher standard of living than is known in much of the world. They will be content as long as they set their minds on things above.

In this example, the fruits of obedience are further evidenced in Dad. He adheres to Scriptural principles of hard work and diligence, and God has rewarded him accordingly—markedly with each birth, by his own testimony. And the fruit can continue to bear many seasons later. A larger family impels Dad to work harder to earn enough money for basic needs and to utilize his wife at home, where her potential family contribution is optimized. The hard work, in turn, enhances his skills and efficiency. It may eventually place him in a position of greater stewardship and greater monetary gain than would have been possible had he not been challenged. Both parents will have the incentive to train their children in household chores and, as soon as possible, in paying jobs. (This process is discussed in more detail in chapter 8.)

The faith of this couple is foundational for their attitude about childbearing. Like a muscle, their faith has been strengthened through exercise—in this case during the additions of their first children. Now they are willing and eager to exercise it further. They appreciate God's blessings in their lives, including the blessing of children. And, remaining obedient to God and His Word, they rightfully expect blessings to increase.

Check Out the Fallow Ground

Proverbs 13:23 says, "Abundant food is in the fallow ground of the poor." That food may well be God's blessing, but He probably does not plan on breaking up the ground, planting, weeding, and harvesting to make the blessing come to reality.

Likewise, God makes abundant provision for families, but, more often than not, they must do their part to see it manifest. They must break up the fallow, or idled, land and reap what can be reaped.

Danny and Nancy Crandall, for example, had five to seven children during the early 1980s. While

Crandall was in school full time, the family lived on veteran's benefits of $400 a month plus $200 a month from a part-time job.

"During those years I discovered all sorts of ways to save money," said Mrs. Crandall. She grew a garden and canned vegetables. She tore up rags to use when they couldn't afford toilet paper.

By 1988, things were starting to level off financially. Crandall, a physicist, expected to earn about $45,000 that year. However, they then had nine children, and found that managing a large family was still a financial and organizational challenge.

So how did they cope?

Each older child had to clean his or her bedroom plus another room before going to school. Mrs. Crandall stacked newly washed clothes on shelves in the laundry room labeled for each child, who then retrieved his or her own clothes. A fourteen-year-old son had a paper route; another son cared for younger siblings while Mrs. Crandall ran errands after school. The older kids also handled dishwashing and were quite self-sufficient, said their mother. "When they want something, they earn the money to buy it. They always can find jobs mowing lawns, pulling weeds, picking berries, cleaning houses; in a big family, you learn how to work."[3]

How do other large families plow their fallow ground?[4]

• A father of eleven in Kingston, New York, says they have a Sunday night planning session to arrange menus, driving schedules, and assign chores. The children do most of the housework, leaving mother free to be "an interested, caring, involved and nurturing mother."

• Shopping only once a month for bulk food and filling a freezer, pantry and fifteen shelves in the garage helps economize, says a father of nine in Reno, Nevada.

• A mother of seven in Birmingham, Alabama, arranges fifteen-minute blocks in the evening for each child so they can discuss homework or anything else on their minds.

• The children help pay for family trips, says a mother of six in Los Angeles, California. Anyone who earns money, such as by babysitting or cutting lawns, puts ten percent into the vacation fund.

• A family with six children in Birmingham puts a condition on teenagers who get their driver's license. They can use the family car, but they must also run errands and chauffeur siblings.

• A mother of six in Steamboat Springs, Colorado, swaps with a friend in caring for each other's preschoolers one day a week while the older kids are in school.

• After getting younger children to bed, a father of six in St. Peters, Missouri, hires his thirteen-year-old to babysit so Mom and Dad can leave for an hour, even if it's just to take a walk.

Keep the Incubator Plugged In

No two families are alike. What works in one family may not work in yours. And certainly, no two spouses (thank the Lord!) are alike. The measure of faith allotted, the maturity of obedience—these will like-wise differ from couple to couple, from spouse to spouse, in quality and quantity. But they should, in a natural way, help determine the size of a family. During that process of building a family, God simply calls us to remain open before Him and endeavor to grow in Christlike qualities. 2 Peter 1:5-8 says this about the maturing process:

> "...applying all diligence, in your faith supply moral excellence, and in your moral excellence, knowledge; and in your knowledge, self-control, and in your self-control, perseverance, and in your perseverance, godliness; and in your godliness, brotherly kindness, and in your brotherly kindness, Christian love. For if these qualities are yours *and are increasing* they render you neither useless nor unfruitful in the true knowledge of our Lord Jesus Christ" (italics added).

Ever heard of building a better mousetrap? It refers to a principle of business success: choosing a venture that offers something better than what anyone else is offering.

Parents have the opportunity for success in their family by building a better incubator. How? First, purpose to make sure the qualities of faith and obedience are yours and are increasing. Second, be diligent to make the most of your fallow ground. By doing these things, your home will be an incubator growing in capacity for Christian babies, who will become baby Christians. They will have a much better chance of maturing as mighty men and women of faith, clear blessings in every phase of their lives.

PART 1

THE PRIVATE PICTURE

SEVEN

MOTHERHOOD: THE NEGLECTED CAREER

> *But women shall be preserved through the bearing of children if they continue in faith and love and sanctity with self-restraint.*
>
> 1 Timothy 2:15

She's a $60,000-a-year executive for Aetna Life and Casualty Insurance of Hartford, Connecticut, said the 1981 *Life* magazine article. Her devotion to her job, as well as wheeling and dealing in real estate on the side, is consuming, "like an obsessive love affair." She is thirty-six, childless, divorced for seven years. She sees little of her "man of the moment." Which may be all for the best since she's not foolish enough, in her words, to be "giving it all up to iron shirts."

This is Janet, Superwoman No. 4837, in the continuing series, courtesy of American media. Superwomen come in two varieties: Brazenly Barren and

Courageously Coping. They are nice for selling women's magazines. And they are positively venomous when it comes to spreading the ideological terrorism that targets contented women and motherhood.

Brazenly Barren, like Janet, is perhaps the most idolized. BB is like a rocket ship: sleek, powerful, unencumbered, moving fast, headed for the stars. She is the unattached executive in TV commercial-land who invites the man, spur of the moment as they collect their mail, to help her "break in" her new Yuppie-class VISA card with the zillion-dollar credit limit. No husband, and more important, *no children* to weigh down this guided missile.

Courageously Coping retains as much character as possible from BB. The difference is that she has to cope with children, and perhaps that dangling appendage that her superwoman evolution has failed to shed: the husband. Those who have found themselves without husband but still with children are automatically courageously coping, whether or not they fancy themselves as superwomen. After all, most single mothers have no choice about entering the work force.

Many married mothers do have a choice. Feminists and progressive media produce a constant stream of articles, books, classes, and seminars to help them with that choice. These mothers are made to feel guilty if they fail to shift into passing gear and join the fast-lane breed of Courageously Coping. With executive-like finesse, women are told, CC schedules her token child or two into her busy day, or more commonly, into a fraction of her night.

"It's not the *quantity* of time—it's the *quality* of the time that counts," she says of her hyper-minutes as Mommy. Readers nod agreeably, failing to call the bluff on this self-justifying malarkey. Not so with the tender young ones who must endure the strange places and changing faces that fill the long hours of day care, school, or empty homes between the magic inoculations of "quality time." In the end, there is little to employ but such verbal sleight-of-hand in trying to bridge the wide gap between Working Woman and Momma.

Tough Questions

Janet and all the other BBs and CCs, even with their driving ambition and achievements, are in many ways no different from the mere mortals who read about them. Women want respect. Women want fulfillment. Women want material security. And most women, though some are slow to admit it, want to have babies and be good mothers.

But how do they satisfy those needs? Relatives and friends, media, and conscience—every source has a different remedy. Complicating that cacophony are a few outright lies.

One of the worst fibs is that motherhood, especially apart from some challenging job, can no longer meet those basic needs of respect, fulfillment, and security. It is a cruel irony of our times that the task of mothering is considered not real work when any fool knows that skilled nurturing is both difficult and in great demand. When hard-working home-based mothers are embarrassed to admit to a new acquaintance that they are "just a housewife," not even baseball and apple pie are safe.

Another damaging falsehood is the whitewash of "obsessive love affairs" with a career (and this goes for men, too). Scripture commands service to an employer to be done heartily, as unto the Lord. But to try to satisfy through work a personal void that would more naturally be filled through self-sacrificial service as a mother or father is futile. An employer is a fickle lover; when your offering is depleted, the affair is over. This is conditional love. And by Scripture's definition, conditional love is no love at all.

For a variety of reasons, American women, including mothers, have rushed to the work place in record numbers. In 1950 only one in eight mothers with children under six was in the work force. Today more than half of them are working outside of the home.[1] Looking at women ages eighteen to forty-nine, about ninety percent of them are in the labor force at some time during any two-year period.[2]

One cannot blame women for clawing their way into every male-dominated niche they could find. Men have come to seek fulfillment in career, wealth, power, personal comforts, alcohol, and drugs—anything besides being an effective husband and father, as God has called them to be. When men abdicate their positions in the home to pursue status outside the home, it immediately downgrades the status of their partners at home. When motherhood and home care become low-ranking livelihoods, no sane woman wants to pursue them. Neglected by her husband and belittled by society, she opts to compete with men. She would risk losing that competition rather than stay home where there is no reward, not even any approbation, for giving herself to the challenging career of motherhood.

I can't blame her. Children are no blessing in this value system. And caring for them without the support of husband, church, and relatives is an unceasing burden.

Women will always work, and they should. But will a woman find greater blessing through paid outside work or through work at home with children? Can a stay-at-home mother really be fulfilled? And what does the Bible say about a woman's calling with regard to having children?

Hey, It's Not So Bad

You've heard that the grass is always greener. Feminists have heard it too. They've played it to the hilt when comparing the "liberation" of careerism versus the drudgery of home-based mothers. The unemployed mother, the story goes, is isolated, bored, and tired from doing housework, a slave to demeaning child care, and, frequently, a dullard growing even duller as she watches daytime soaps and plays a pretty pet parrot to decorate the walls of her husband's life.

This is another myth. In his insightful book *Men and Marriage*, George Gilder cites studies by Herbert J. Gans and Helen Znaniecki Lopata that found women actually enjoy suburban life and are well-rounded and involved outside their homes. The findings of the two researchers depict a panorama of social engagement, community concern, cooperative activity, and even, in many cases, cultural and intellectual animation: a realm of options that substantially exceeds those of either men or working women. Mrs. Lopata, for instance, found that suburban housewives, by a significant margin, were more likely than working women to be using their education in their lives, to be reading widely and curiously, to be maintaining close and varied friendships, and to be involved in community affairs....Working women normally looked forward to leaving their jobs. Gans found that only ten percent of suburban women reported frequent loneliness or boredom.[3]

Motherhood plays no small part in this. The shepherding of children from cribs through college ties a mother into several interpersonal webs with fellow mothers in the neighborhood, church, and school. Because of children, she may find herself at the library, the zoo, the soccer game, the park, the art exhibit, the concert, the theater, the school board meeting, or any number of other educational, cultural, or even political organizations.

She might even find herself dodging cottonmouths. One summer day my wife spoke on the phone to the mother of a neighborhood boy who, along with Aaron, our eldest son, had been looking for snakes (and finding them!) in a nearby creek.

"I'd give *anything* to be catching snakes out there with them!" moaned this mother, speaking from her job.

This mother is single. She has to work. A married woman whose career revolves around caring for her family, though, has no allegiance to an employer. She has that much more time and energy to give to her friends and associates, to her church and her hobbies, and most importantly, to her husband and children. In the sense that motherhood can be a satisfying, well-rounded, even exciting livelihood, children are a blessing for their mother.

Of course, it's a transparent blessing to those who've most loudly told women their pot of gold lies in the work world. Let's review the agenda of those who've encouraged American women to postpone, neglect, or totally forget the blessing of children in favor of joining the work force. There's more at stake than just prestige and a paycheck.

A Woman's Place

The most authentic American superwoman lived around colonial times. She was light-years away from Brazenly Barren; the average woman in 1776 married between ages eighteen and twenty and bore seven to ten children.[4] And her performance ranked well above Courageously Coping. Even with hubby and all those kids, early American women actually had broad, highly involved social roles. They were active in business, politics, the army, the ministry, and the arts.[5] Business tended to be simpler, centered in or near the home, so women and children played a more vital role in that sphere without inflicting the damages of parent-absence.

The Industrial Revolution changed all that. It began to erode the traditional link between home and labor, eventually devaluing the immediate economic worth of children. The process continues to this day, as evidenced by the loss of family farms. As industrialization took root in the nineteenth century, men went further from home to work. Sexual divisions evolved in the new kinds of employment, so that "women's work" and "men's work" were more clearly defined.

This blossoming of capitalism, with its many opportunities for wealth and risk-taking, not only drew men away from home, but away from God, notes Carl Wilson in his book *Our Dance Has Turned to Death*. In their pursuit of the idol mammon, men had little time for God or godly responsibilities toward family.[6] Wives frequently found themselves alone. Children, in some of the larger cities, were hideously abused as they became virtual slaves in factories. The only blessing they constituted was the meager paycheck they brought home.

There was, however, a social and corporate consciousness to preserve the family during this upheaval. In the early nineteenth century, the writings of Catharine Beecher called for keeping the home a moral greenhouse and a sanctuary from the work place in order to preserve religion and the family. The family illustrated God's heavenly kingdom, and the woman, refraining from leaving it for paid labor, was its chief minister.

The Family Wage

Another indication of this age's pro-child underpinnings was the "family wage," or living wage. This was a concept that heads of households, who were almost always males, deserved higher wages in order to support their families. The idea had not always been necessary. Prior to the emergence of the Industrial Revolution, children were more clearly economic assets to their family. They could work together with the family on its farm or other enterprise and later provide security for parents in their old age.

When this old order was turned topsy-turvy, there was suddenly an unfairness to having and raising children. Why should one couple be considerably more burdened with child-related costs than another couple? It was in this vein that family wage became a major social, political and religious issue, and remained so for much of the last two centuries. The term's present obscurity testifies to how much feminists and other anti-family warriors have won in the battle to coerce women away from child care and into the labor market.

The idea of the family wage, then, was not to be unfair to working women, but to protect the moral-economic order in which children were desired and properly nurtured. The trial and error of centuries had shown that family was the basic social unit and that men and women functioned at their optimum when sex roles were distinct. Unduly high wages for women could discourage young women from marriage and motherhood; for others, it could lure them away from the home, where their skills could be most highly utilized, especially in caring for children.[7]

The family wage concept is pretty radical stuff for today. Yet in its heyday, it was supported not by conservatives, but by the dominant wing of last century's feminist movement.

Advocates linked the "social feminist" emphasis on the importance of motherhood and the family with the historic trade union emphasis on the dignity and independence of the male breadwinner. As the slogan of the Women's Trade Union League, the primary organization of working women, put it: "The eight-hour day; a living wage; to guard the home."[8]

"Guarding the home," then, was a noble calling. To have to abandon this critical command post for bondage to factory work, or some other common job, was a raw deal.

The next century, though, saw this prevailing attitude fade as the capitalist expansion continued. By the turn of the century, households became consuming units instead of the productive units they once were. As the family business left the home, wives and children were less important as a source of labor. The miracles of technology—dishwashers, vacuum cleaners, and the like—along with vastly improved food distribution and storage, and smaller household size, further devalued the home-economic worth of the housewife and children. With increasing job specialization brought about by the maturing industrial age, it became critical for children to invest themselves as full-time students rather than as unskilled labor.

Many women were drawn into the labor market by the special demands of World War II. Following the war, there were new incentives for women to work as millions of new jobs required "domestic skills," such as teaching, social work, nursing and clerical work.[9]

Then, for the first time, the federal government threw its weight behind working women. President Dwight Eisenhower called the 1955 White House Conference on the Effective Use of Womanpower. Speakers there articulated women's demands and prophesied the coming wave of female employment.

Feminists had done an about-face, and few people seemed to care. Home was out; outside work was in. Woman was no longer the indispensable guardian of the hearth, as described by earlier feminists, but a mere competitor with men in the newly glamorized world of work. Those sounding the siren call for women to join the work force had betrayed the most basic urge of woman, motherhood, and its accompanying high calling of ministry in the home. The shift demoted children several points lower on the blessing-burden scale.

Treasonous Sisters

This is not to say that everything should have stayed as it was in 1776, or in Jesus' day, or in Old Testament times. Home economy and society had changed drastically and irreversibly, at least in industrialized nations. It was logical that more women, having fewer children and no household commercial enterprise to care for, would seek paid work away from home. And it's fair that employers no longer attempt to pay on a selective basis a so-called "family wage." To do so today would discriminate against a sizable proportion of unmarried workers, both male and female.

But even with these profound societal changes, the treason of the new breed of feminists was inexcusable because they denied core principles basic to femininity. Concerning the home with an available mother as the best place for children to find a shelter, a training ground and a source of love and identity, little had changed: for children age six and above, only formal education had intervened; for the preschoolers, those most in need of megadoses of Momma, nothing had changed.

Equally vicious in this treason was the disregard for women, the alleged victims. Those whose most innate sense of identity is bound up with fertility were encouraged to abandon, delay, or at least severely limit childbearing. They were asked to deny their deepest biological and psychological urges toward maternity for the sake of a paycheck. They were told to rejoice at "liberation" from the home, which their ancestors gained deep satisfaction in maintaining. In other words, they were supposed to squash every feminine impulse that pulsated for expression.

Media stories began trickling out in the 1980s about women who bought the lie and wanted their money back. Many discovered, pathetically, that they waited too late to conceive; or even to tie down a mate who would stick around long enough to be called Daddy; or that Daddy took advantage of the spirit of women's liberation and liberated himself from all family responsibilities. And those lucky enough to accumulate both husband and children along the career path found work wasn't all it was cracked up to be. Two-thirds of mothers working full time would rather be working fewer hours so they could be with their families more.[10]

This chronic unfulfillment of the modern woman has been a major theme over the last decade in the weekly reader-written "Hers" column in the *New York Times*, as analyzed by teacher/editor Carol Iannone. The varied columns include ones

> that bewail the loss of intimacy in women's lives, that attack the Superwoman syndrome....Some women long for a baby, others admit they'd like a man, while still others have had it with the new sensitive male and the new hands-on daddy. Those who don't have it all wish they did, but those who do have it all seem to be missing something still.[11]

Surprise, surprise, surprise. The unscathed Courageously Coping and the totally fulfilled Brazenly Barren were make-believe all along. For too many women, these models were cruel myths.

The Feminist Agenda

It's no secret that women are flooding the job market, delaying marriage and motherhood, and getting divorced in record numbers. What's less apparent is the feminist theology that has in part driven such changes.

So let's look at just one of the extreme goals held by some architects of the new woman: androgyny. This refers to a blurring of the sex roles. It means men being more like women, and women acting like men.

Androgyny is critical to shooting down the traditional esteem placed on motherhood, so consequently the spiritual and emotional worth of children goes down in flames with it. Where androgyny is emerging, other things must be fading. Pregnancy, as distinctively feminine and carrying its share of discomforts, falls into disrepute. Child-raising, a major inconvenience to women aspiring to male-female equality in the business-political towers, is jettisoned. Motherhood, a new victim status tied to the old "patriarchal" tyranny, is absolutely loathed. Under this ideology, children are clearly liabilities, and the state is the one to dump them on.

Speaking more out front than some of her feminist sisters, Shulamith Firestone, in her 1979 book about feminist revolution, spared no sweet talk about the need for total family upheaval. Allan Carlson of the Rockford Institute describes how she attributed the collapse of Russia's Communist revolution to

> its failure to destroy utterly the family, which was the true source of psychological, economic, and political oppression. Day care and equality in pay and jobs were not enough. Capitalist tokenism was a lie and a sham, she said: "Mom is vital to the American way of life, considerably more than apple pie. She is an institution without which the system really *would* fall apart." Hence, "Mom" must be eliminated, to be supplanted by a "feminist socialism" that would end capitalist exploitation (author's italics).[12]

This, of course, involved the usual utopian menu: state nurseries and high-techno-pediatrics such as cloning and bottle-fed babies—anything to separate woman from motherhood. And that's not all. The same moral base that longs to make traditional maternity obsolete also looks forward to freeing women *and children* for unrestricted sex play to help humanity revert to "its natural 'polymorphously perverse' sexuality."[13] In other words, the revolution would, in the long run, necessitate breaking down male/female and adult/child distinctions for a final victory of glorious androgyny.

This radically unbalanced perspective—the attack on motherhood, the merging of sex roles, the obvious disregard for sacrificial nurturance—is not uncommon among feminist ideologues. The ideas they try to pawn as "progressive" often reflect their personal failure to progress to a state of normal, mature femininity. Dr. Harold M. Voth, the psychiatrist and psychoanalyst, writes:

> The family backgrounds of many of the well-known militant women's liberationists are the classical variants from the norm. Virtually all of them present evidence which suggests a breakdown in the mother-child relationship and an unresolved attachment either to a weak, remote or at times tyrannical father. *These women really seek liberation from these adult responsibilities which only mature, feminine women can assume and upon which the future of mankind depends. The liberationists quite naturally seek to alter the most fundamental fabric of society so as to accommodate their psychopathology which has led to their value system.* One feminist put it most suc-

cinctly when she said, "We do not seek equality but superiority. We are becoming the men we wanted to marry"[14] (italics added).

Admittedly, pure androgyny and rampant kiddie sex remain on the periphery of today's liberal value spectrum (though it is not hard to find more than traces of both). Even many self-described feminists today would not subscribe to such a level of revolution that would deliver the final punch to the already reeling and bleeding American family.

The point is that ideas have consequences. Revolutions in birth control, fertility, and women's roles—as well as other social upheavals including divorce, abortion, child pornography and exploitation, open homosexuality, drug abuse, and militant secularism—had their prophets. The prophets found followers. The followers have acted. And they have moved with enough determination, in areas such as abortion and secular humanism, to get their fringe ideologies codified in law that affects the masses.

So today we are seeing what might be called the first fruits of aggressive anti-natalism—for example, legal abortion and below-replacement birth rates since the early 1970s, and a sizable wave of bitter, often barren, female workers. The autumn fruits will be worse. Studies are showing that so many of today's children— those ignored by careerist parents, those raised in father-absent homes, and those lacking basic moral foundations—will yield even more broken homes and scarred children.

Jesus said you would know the tree by its fruits. Let's examine a different tree and its fruits.

Fertility and Work

We saw in chapters 3 and 4 that procreation and motherhood were high on God's agenda in the Old Testament. The New Testament lacks that same punch. It doesn't have anything like the extended narratives found in Genesis that develop the theme of a chosen people destined to have a census count like the stars of heaven. The New Testament, though, incorporates general Old Testament perspectives, as shown in Jesus' statement that He came to fulfill the Law and the Prophets (Matt. 5:17). And it does present a few endorsements of women having babies.

Even so, there remains a vast middle ground to negotiate, especially for young mothers, between Brazenly Barren and the home-based mother of three preschoolers. Should I work full time? Part time? Outside the home? Only before children are born? Only when there are no preschoolers? Only after they've completely left the nest? Should I even have any children? Or wait till I'm thirty-five? How many should I have?

The Bible does not directly answer those questions. But it does provide some guidelines in two broad areas that cover those queries: What God desires for married women regarding fertility and work. With a foundation established there, a husband and wife can more fully weigh career and childbirth choices to determine if anything is interfering with God's calling on the wife.

Childbearing Affirmed

We've seen that while marriage was considered a command for the Jews, it received a less enthusiastic endorsement from the early church. Marriage and procreation shared top billing with a high regard for virginity, perhaps reflecting a current, Greek-influenced obsession to suppress carnality. Still, the general Hebrew outlook of contra-contraception and pro-procreation was carried over in the church. The apostle Paul was quite clear:

"But women shall be preserved (or saved, or kept safe) through the bearing of children if they continue in faith and love and sanctity with self-restraint" (1 Tim. 2:15).

Try that verse on your local National Organization of Women chapter and see if you leave without powder burns around your ears. The verse is so out front that it almost seems to fall off the page. At least, one might surmise, it's mistranslated.

It's not.

Ex-feminist Mary Pride, in her book *The Way Home*, clarifies the verse by pointing out its context. It follows Paul's instruction on how men should pray and women should dress, and his equally radical statements that a woman should "quietly receive instruction with entire submissiveness" (2:11), and should not teach the church or exert authority over men (2:12).

The next logical question would be, "Well, then, what *can* women do for God if they are

not supposed to teach?" Paul says that by per-
severing in our God-given role—childbearing—with a godly attitude, we will be saved.
"Childbearing" sums up all our special biological and domestic functions. This is the
exact same grammatical construction as
Paul's advice to Timothy that Timothy should
persevere in his life and doctrine, "because if
you do, you will save both yourself and your
hearers" (1 Tim. 4:16). Timothy's particular
path to heavenly glory was his preaching and
example. Ours is homeworking, all revolving
around our role of childbearing.[15]

"Saved" in this passage, of course, is not the same
as salvation through Jesus Christ. Mrs. Pride quotes
Greek scholar A.T. Robertson, who says women will
be saved "in this function, not by means of it." And
she cites James Hurley as paraphrasing "Paul as saying women in general (and most women in his day)
will be kept safe from seizing men's roles by partici-
pating in marital life (symbolized by childbirth)...."[16]

Sounds like Paul felt men were a little threatened,
doesn't it? Not really. Paul is highlighting that it is
normal and good for men and women to have different roles, to excel in them, and not move toward what
we would call androgyny.

In the same epistle, Paul advises younger widows to
get married, have children, and manage their homes
(1 Tim. 5:14). There is no reason to think that marriage, maternity, and diligent home management are
remedial callings unique to widowhood. Rather they
describe the normal state of affairs for women, a

more edifying livelihood than being aimless "gossips and busybodies" (5:13).

Discontentment and Idolatry

So far we have seen that the unbroken thrust of Scripture is that God smiles on marriage and procreation. His Word says women find their fulfillment in becoming mothers. So does work outside the home interfere with priorities related to motherhood and home care?

Again, individual circumstances vary so greatly that it would be wrong to issue a blanket condemnation of mothers who leave children and home to work. A single mother generally has no choice. In an intact family, financial need or a father's personal problems can force a mother onto someone's payroll.

But exactly what constitutes a need that *requires* a mother to bring home a second paycheck? Everyone's standard of living differs. And you won't find a clear Bible verse telling you whether you need one car or two or three, or how new they should be, or if it's OK for them to have five-hundred-dollar audio systems, or whether it's God's will for you to take on a mortgage for a modest vacation home at the beach.

What you can find in the Bible is a little pearl you'd probably rather not discover. It's another directive in the first epistle to Timothy: "And if we have food and covering (clothing, not housing) with these we shall be content" (6:8). Paul goes on to expound that "the love of money is a root of all sorts of evil" (6:10) and that the godly man should instead chase after righteousness, godliness, faith, love, perseverance and gentleness (6:11). The passage does not mean that it's sin to possess more than crusty bread and a few dusty cloaks or to have a personal savings plan. It does say that discontentment is sin, and that money can become an idol. A mother considering work strictly to bring in extra income needs to consider, along with her husband, their motive. Are they operating strictly from a foundation of discontentment or money-worship? If so, they may need to back off the second paycheck. The Bible requires them to have an attitude of contentment as long as they are able to meet basic needs.

Home: Castle or Prison?

The paycheck, of course, is not the only motive for mothers seeking employment. Many want not just a job, but a career, an exciting track for fulfilling self-potential. They also want an escape from the confines of housework and child care. Mrs. Pride examines several Bible figures who at times have been cited as noteworthy examples of working women: Deborah, Priscilla, Lydia, Hannah, Sarah, Mary, and the Proverbs mother. The author finds no Scriptural endorsement of what the modern world would consider careerist wives, though many of them obviously were productive within their own realm.[17]

One reason many of those examples did not fit the career mold is that their roles were home-based. So the related consideration in studying roles for mothers is the Scriptural perspective of mothers at home versus mothers outside the home.

Proverbs 31 provides an especially graphic portrait of a happy, busy woman. She stays up late and rises early. She cooks, plants, and crafts. Those activities are at least partially directed toward the needs of children, though this is no woman overcome by repetitive child care duties. The passage indicates she is involved with her husband, her maidens, and the poor, not to mention the "tradesmen" and other merchants with whom she must deal. Yet the overall impression is that of a woman who is based in her home, who "looks well to the ways of her household" (31:27), apparently before meeting outside needs. And she's good at it and fully satisfied—her children and her husband speak highly of her; even her works bring her praise at the city gates.

The work-at-home image of the Proverbs mother is further emphasized in Titus 2. Paul tells Titus what older women should teach young women: "to love their husbands, to love their children, to be sensible, pure, *workers at home*, kind, being subject to their own husbands, that the Word of God may not be dishonored" (2:4-5, italics added).

The general outline for the priorities of young women, then, is that they are to be maternal and home-centered. Paul assumes that young women usually have children, and their needs and those of the husband are to be paramount to the lady of the house. The only reference to work is that it is at home. The NIV Bible translates "workers at home" as *busy at home*.

Build on the Foundation

There is, therefore, a strong Scriptural endorsement for women to bear children and center their lives around the home. What is lacking here is any specific prohibition. To say that it's absolutely wrong for married women, or mothers, or mothers of preschoolers to be employed out of the home is just as fallacious as a pronouncement that every use of contraception is wrong. Committed Christian couples seeking God's heart on these matters may very well find a burden of conscience that says two incomes would be wrong. But an explicit law for mothers working outside the home? It's simply not in the Bible.

Rather, Christians must be grounded in the Bible's value system: Marriage, motherhood, and women vigorously caring for the home are good. What the neighbor women are doing, what's discussed on Phil Donahue's show, what the latest poll of women in *USA Today* shows—these should not play determining roles in the unfolding of a married woman's calling.

The statistics of modern family breakdown speak of countless tragedies where the blind are leading the blind. The blind leaders are undergirded by ideologies that level the differences between male and female, that destroy traditional family, that reject Christianity and its patriarchal emphases, and that applaud diminished fertility.

Those whose eyes have been opened by the authentic women's Liberator need not tread the path of the blind. Christian mothers may find a clear conscience to work with great zest outside the home. But those who've entered into a love relationship with Christ must guard their hearts against playing the whore through an "obsessive love affair" with a job.

Christ offers a love relationship lacking nothing in the way of fulfillment, security, and contentment. A woman who has carefully aligned herself with God's foundational order will be at peace in whatever roles she is called to fill, including the exalted role of mother.

EIGHT

PARENTHOOD'S DEEP
CURRENTS OF BLESSING

> *She opens her mouth in wisdom, and
> the teaching of kindness is on her
> tongue.*
>
> (Proverbs 31:26).

> *A worker's appetite works for him, for
> his hunger urges him on.*
>
> Proverbs 16:26

"They wanted us to let her die," said Mack.
"They said she wouldn't live through the
night."

The doctors told Mack and Janice, friends
of mine, not to use life support systems with their
newborn daughter.

Elizabeth, their second daughter, had just been
delivered by cesarean section six weeks premature.
She was afflicted with trisomy-13, a rare chromoso-
mal defect. Elizabeth had an extra finger on both
hands, unformed eyes and a severe cleft palate. She
was underweight and probably had no hearing. Her
heart was defective. Her brain was missing.

If Elizabeth survived the first twenty-four hours, she would have a life expectancy of three months. The doctors felt she could not, or should not, survive those twenty-four hours.

"Something rose up in me," Mack said. "I said, 'You're making a decision that's mine. God brought this child into the world and I want her alive until He decides to take her back.'"

The doctors rallied behind Mack and Janice. Elizabeth lived five and a half months, and even spent a good portion of that time at home with her family.

To the casual observer, she was a physical, emotional, and financial burden from day one. To her parents, as we will examine later, she was a source of blessings that are worth more and will last longer than blessings that come with a price tag.

Though Elizabeth had a rare physical condition, she was ordinary in that she brought change in her parents. Every child does. The issue for husbands and wives is how they embrace their new (or expanding) status as parents. Is your perspective geared toward sacrifice (sowing) for future reward (reaping)? Or is it merely coping with a burden that God has dumped on you?

We take for granted the process by which young adults mate, bear offspring, and work willingly to support their families. Yet there is a delicate balance: subtract children, and the cycle collapses. Childless couples may still hold jobs, but the effort they put into work, what they do with their earnings, how they spend their time—these differ from the choices of their parenting neighbors. Children are blessings to adults who conceived them, in part because the little ones, whether born with health and plentiful skills or handicapped to the point of uselessness, force a fuller maturity on their caretakers. In turn, the maturing parents form a more stable community and nation as they steward the stewards of tomorrow.

From Wives to Mothers

We've seen that much of the ideology behind the modern exodus of women to the work force desires to homogenize men's and women's roles. What has suffered most is not men's egos, but motherhood and children. Fertility is under attack. Its foes deem as anachronistic platitude the Bible's apparent bias toward home-based motherhood as woman's highest calling.

Following Scripture's commands and examples relating to the role of women can be quite difficult today. That obedience, which may require the sacrifice of a rewarding career or other outlets for external stimulation, carries its own reward for Christians because obedience pleases God.

Yet even beyond that reward, there are physical benefits that accrue to women who choose to bear children. Certain health studies bear out the truth of 1 Timothy 2:15, "women shall be preserved through the bearing of children." For example, women who breast-feed their babies have a lower incidence of breast cancer. One study shows that mothers over fifty may be at lower risk for sudden, fatal heart attacks than childless women of the same age.[1]

While many couples wishing to have children are infertile, others are barren by choice, needlessly subjecting the woman to potential health problems with regard to prolonged menstruation. Married women are, for the first time in history, able to menstruate thirteen times a year for most of their adult life if they continue practicing birth control. These are indications that an unceasing menstrual cycle can put damaging stress on a woman's system, particularly on the breasts. Cancer of the ovary and other parts seems to be more prevalent in women who avoid childbirth.[2]

Once a child arrives, a woman's identity broadens. Whether she works full time, part time, or not at all outside the home, the addition of a screaming love sponge challenges her to new heights. The residence is no longer merely a comfy pad where one can relax, eat, and entertain friends. Suddenly it becomes a training camp. Tomorrow's carpenters are trying to hammer nails into your refinished hardwood floor. Tomorrow's secretaries are practicing crayon shorthand on your walls. Tomorrow's athletes are slithering across the floor and climbing onto tables. Tomorrow's stockbrokers are arguing over items ransomed from the garbage. Tomorrow's labor negotiators are beating each other with pillows torn from the couch. Tomorrow's ministers are memorizing filthy rhymes learned from the neighborhood kids.

If there were ever a place to put Christianity to practice, this is it. These young creatures need a flesh-and-blood extension of God's love. They need training in righteousness. They need a place of solace, of rest. They need a righteous judge. They need order in the court. They need a healer. They need a friend.

They need a storyteller. They need a visage of stature, God's beauty personified.

They need a mother. And they need her a lot.

They need a home, too, made and ordered with deliberate care.

Children, of course, need fathers, too. Fathers do meet many of those basic needs, as well as others. But women possess a special calling that springs from their unique creation. And they are generally more accessible than fathers.

My wife, Edie, was home caring for our three sons one August when neighborhood boys, some of them close to junior high age, drifted into our den. One confided that it was the first day he had been out all summer.

"Out?" my wife asked.

He explained that he had stayed inside, watching soap operas.

The blessing was flowing both ways in our den. My wife, just by being home and friendly, was a brief joy to budding young men who normally would rather do anything than chat with a friend's mother. She enjoyed a frank talk with the youngsters, some of whom had never dropped by. None of this could have happened if she had not been available.

This sort of occurrence triggers the child-blessing for Edie, who is gifted in teaching and befriending children. The bigger our quiver is, the more she is drawn into her calling within her own home and the more chances she gets to exercise her gifting with others in need.

Other women may not feel particularly gifted in relation to teaching children, but they undoubtedly have other spiritual giftings if they have surrendered their lives to Christ. Many such callings or talents can be expressed in some way through the home.

Besides, every woman has a basic deposit of femininity that is part of the Master's design. Women who remain barren may never touch vast portions of what it means to be female. As deep as the bond can be between two spouses, the mother-child relationship is for many women even deeper and more fulfilling than loving a man. Maternity ties women to their own mothers, their own daughters, to women of history, with a depth that pales the acclaim or satisfaction that comes from a job or any other source. This is a blessing that cannot be bought.

Yet at the same time, though God places high esteem on fertility, it is certainly not the only means to fulfillment for a woman of God. After all, many married women are infertile; other women are single and beyond their fertile years. God may have withheld the blessing of children, but He is the author of all blessings, and they come in many forms. Women who never become mothers may or may not be pained over their barrenness, but they need never feel cheated by God or spiritually handicapped. As long as they yield themselves to God's purposes for their lives, they should expect no lesser degree of personal fulfillment and overall blessing.

From Men to Fathers

The capability for maternity, in fact, is the dominant physical trait that defines woman. It also means women have a much superior sexuality than do men, argues George Gilder in his book, *Men and Marriage*. Large portions of a woman's adult life can be occupied by matters that are both sexual and related to childbearing—menstruation, pregnancy, lactation, nursing, and intercourse. This last item is the only sexual component for man. And still it is the woman, in many ways, who determines whether men are granted even this experience.

Outside of promiscuous situations, where true love and childbearing are furthest from their minds, men must make commitments to qualify as a sex partner. Marriage, or some similar promise of long-term presence and provision, has historically been the price men pay to win the right to continual sex. Gilder credits women, the very locus of fertility, as being the creators of civilization as they

> transform male lust into love; channel male wanderlust into jobs, homes and families; link men to specific children; rear children into citizens; change hunters into fathers; divert male will to power into a drive to create. Women conceive the future that men tend to flee; they feed the children that men ignore.[3]

"Settle down and get married" may be a cliche, but it is also a powerful metamorphosis. When I first met Edie, I was a carousing college student, about to leave for a summer of working and hitchhiking around Europe. I planned the following summer to work in New York City, which I did, and was toying with plans that after graduation I would hitchhike across Canada and the Western United States, avoiding work and seeking good times.

I would be discounting the work of God if I did not acknowledge that accepting Christ about a year before my graduation made a mess of my values and plans. But working at the same time was a process as old as God's creation: domestication.

Most husbands could tell similar versions of my story. For some bachelors, marriage means giving up a bevy of girlfriends. For others, it means fewer nights nursing cool beers with the boys. But for every man, marriage is something of a business deal: He sacrifices something to get something of more value. Gilder says

> the self-sacrifice of women finds a perfect complement in the self-sacrifice of men. On this mutual immolation is founded the fulfillment of human civilization and happiness. For just as it is the sacrifice of early career ambitions and sexual freedom that makes possible the true fulfillment of women, it is the subordination of male sexuality to woman's maternity that allows the achievement of male career goals, that spurs the attainment of the highest male purposes. In his vaunted freedom and sexual power, the young single man may dream of glory. But it is overwhelmingly the married men who achieve it in the modern world. They achieve it, as Scripture dictates and women's experience insists, by self-denial and sacrifice.[4]

As we know too well, the age-old domestication process of marriage can falter. Couples can now cohabit without commitment or society's sneer.

Divorce is much more prevalent and acceptable. Increasing childlessness makes both shacking up and divorce much more tolerable. The feminist revolution has made it much easier for men to flee. Children and, ironically, women are the losers in all this.

On the positive side, a man who sticks it out and takes on the responsibility of fatherhood is virtually forced to rearrange furniture—not just physically, but mentally, spiritually, and financially. The man who was willing to trade partying and philandering for the security of one mate, steady sex, good food, and household services now faces a deal that is not so savvy. With no short-term return other than a potential emotional lift, the man is asked to change diapers, to build doll houses, to serve on PTA committees, to attend Little League games, to assist with homework, to assemble swingsets, and to fix bicycles.

This can be bad enough, but the financial costs are staggering. The good father is required to save for his children's education and perhaps other needs. Sooner or later he'll need to buy a larger house. And with the cost of raising just one child estimated at well above $100,000, he can expect to divert a major portion of his income toward someone besides himself. It can puncture those pipe dreams of sports car, ski boat, new shotgun, wide-screen television, or any of the other toys that thrill us grown-up boys.

The good part is that this brings out the best in the man. If he recognizes his family as depending upon his support, and the paycheck doesn't seem to spread around enough, he will push himself to his limits to be a vocational success. He may have to retrain for higher paying work. He may have to change jobs. He will probably have to work harder no matter what job he takes. Studies have shown that an additional child motivates a father to work the equivalent of two to six weeks of work per year.[5] While any prospect of additional work might be construed negatively by some, the voluntary expansion of both family and productivity should normally be a sign of healthy growth.

Responsibility for a family has other effects on a father. A caring father will consciously refrain from foolish activity because his income is limited, his responsibilities unrelenting. He cannot risk his paycheck on exorbitant wagers at the race track or on next weekend's football game. He cannot let alcohol or drugs dominate him, lest he lose the edge in his job, if not his entire career. He cannot indulge in frivolous consumer spending—say, running up a thousand dollars on the credit card for a new stereo system—because debt is ever knocking on the door. He cannot drive as if he were in a movie chase scene because there are other bodies who need his support, who love him as dearly as he loves them.

What is society like when its barbarians (to borrow Gilder's terminology) are domesticated? Employment is higher. Those employed are living straighter, working harder, competing, so the economy expands. Personal savings increase, creating inheritances for future generations (in accord with Proverbs 13:22, "A good man leaves an inheritance for his children's children") and capital for business expansion.

The trend of personal savings in the United States mirrors the transition from man as sacrificial domestic steward to man as barbarian. The savings rate fell from nine percent of after-tax income in the mid-1970s to 5.1 percent in 1985, to 2.8 percent in the third quarter of 1987. This does not stack up well against our thrifty trading partners Japan (fifteen percent) and West Germany (thirteen percent).[6] Americans' lackadaisical attitude about personal savings is a sign of a generation that is rejecting its offspring because there is no faith, no excitement, about the future.

Outside the financial realm, there are other benefits from tamed former bachelors who have accepted responsibility for their children. Look at your churches, non-profit organizations, PTAs, and similar groups. It is fathers and mothers, not single adults, who typically are most involved and providing leadership. This is no accident. They have the most to reap from the success of such groups—the proper socialization of their children and the insurance of a better community in the future.

No Pain, No Gain

Marriage is the first step toward taming the male barbarian, but the rates of divorce and male infidelity show that the wedding bells often are not enough. Parenthood is no guarantee, either, though the addition of children is a definite motivator for men to quit acting like boys.

Unfortunately, as we've seen, parenthood is waning. Of the twenty-nine percent of married women who were childless in 1985, a sizable portion had chosen barrenness. For them and their husbands, unreality tends to creep in. Most such couples nowadays are dual-income and affluent. Their economy of scale by living together (yet without other dependents) often means a surplus of disposable income. If they want, they can continue indefinitely as playboy and play-girl, consuming most of their wealth, saving for nothing more than their own early retirement, living in different cities if it suits them.

Spurning parenthood may be convenient for some couples, but eventually it is more restrictive than the dreaded shackles of having to care for children. Barrenness limits the depth to which a couple will grow, both in the full sense of family and in their maturity as adults, especially adult Christians. Catholic author James Hitchcock said the marriage commitment is sealed by children,

> who forge it in such a way that much more is at stake than merely the desires of two people. It is in becoming parents that we fulfill a particular kind of destiny that God and nature have bestowed on most of us, that we achieve genuine adulthood.[7]

Genuine adulthood—most of us would say we aspire to it, but are we willing to pay the price?

Returning to Mack, Janice, and their baby, Elizabeth, we find a couple who was willing to sacrifice. In five and a half months of sacrificial love, they gained a depth of Christian maturing that eludes most couples for their entire lifetime.

And what is Christian maturity? Avoiding sin has little to do with it. Going to church is certainly no measure of it. Staying busy with Christian ministry may reflect Christian maturity, but it is no proof positive. Rather, Christian maturity is coming to see things more and more as God sees them. It is to be continually "transformed by the renewing of your mind" (Rom. 12:2) in order to gain the mind of Christ.

In this way Elizabeth was an unqualified blessing to her parents. This helpless baby, bordering on death from the moment she came out of the womb, holding no promise of a remotely normal life, taught a rich lesson about God's perspective on the sanctity of life, recalled her mother.

"It's not so much the quality of life that's important," Janice said. Rather, it is life itself, created by God in His own image, that is of absolute value.

Easy to say, harder to practice. Elizabeth's stay in the hospital was trying enough. It meant visiting twice or more per day, seeing no chance of significant improvement, watching the medical bills climb into the thousands of dollars.

But all along, her parents' goal was to have her home so that her entire life would not be confined to the hospital. After about three months, God granted their prayer request. Sacrifice then took on a new meaning.

"It was like a day-to-day battle to keep her alive," Mack said. Elizabeth's condition was so unstable that her heart or lungs would frequently stop. Electric monitors would sound an alarm, and her parents would revive her by various means, whether thumping her foot or giving the chest thrusts of cardio-pulmonary resuscitation. During the weeks she spent at home, she needed resuscitation literally hundreds of times, at all hours of the day and night. Janice could not even go outside in the yard because she never knew when her daughter's vital systems would turn off.

"People say, 'How could you go through that?'" she recalled. "You set your sights and do what you have to do."

This couple found that God rewarded their faith as they trained their thoughts and ordered their lives on the conviction that their baby, unwanted in the eyes of the world, was an unmitigated blessing from God. The most positive reward was constant fellowship with God.

"I didn't have to go off in a corner and pray in tongues for ten minutes," Mack said. "God was in our presence continually. When it was over, it was like we had come out of a five-and-a-half-month revival."

How else did Elizabeth become a blessing for this family?

• "She taught us so much about the unconditional love of the Lord," said Janice. If God extends unconditional love and forgiveness to us no matter who we are and what we've done, how much more we should unconditionally love and nurture those He entrusts to our care.

• She caused her parents' marriage to be strengthened. The literature on coping with a seriously disabled child emphasized that the strains could tear a marriage apart; in their case, it was just the opposite.

• She opened opportunities for witnessing. Doctors, nurses, a social worker, and many others saw faith and godly conviction in action.

• In spite of her death, Elizabeth confirmed God's willingness to heal. When she contracted pneumonia in both lungs during her two months at home, her parents begged the doctors to wait twenty-four hours before deciding to put her in the hospital. Once again, there was prayer for healing that night. An X-ray the next day showed no trace of pneumonia. The doctors confirmed it was a miracle. She stayed at home for another week, in relatively good health, and then died. "It was like the Lord said, 'I just want to show you that I can heal,'" Mack said.

In retrospect, these parents would not have treated their frail daughter any differently. "She was an absolute blessing," said her father.

The sad truth is that Elizabeths in other families can be burdens. They do sometimes fracture marriages. The encouraging truth is that God intends these special children to be blessings, though the blessings may come in different forms from those on which the parents were counting. But they are blessings nevertheless. All God requires is that parents align their appraisals of children with His and be open to receiving *His* blessings.

The gift of children, then, can bless parents immediately. Even though children such as Elizabeth hold no promise of performing work or otherwise producing tangible fruit for society, they stimulate blessings in their parents in the form of growth toward maturity.

Growing, healthy families form tiny building blocks for a society. In transforming women into mothers, men into fathers, families elicit the best potential from both partners. Family formation raises the odds that all players will reach a fuller maturity.

Honing the Child

Not only do parents learn in great depth the meaning of Christian sacrifices, but when there is more than one child, the children, too, learn about sacrifice until the day they leave the nest. What greater training ground than family could exist for children to learn the heart of Philippians 2:3-4? "Do nothing from selfishness or empty conceit, but with humility of mind let each of you regard one another as more important than himself; do not merely look out for your own personal interests, but also for the interests of others."

The only child is unfairly removed from reality. She may go to school and experience the unpleasant side of social interaction, but it is only a sampling of the lions' den of living with siblings. Sharing a classroom with twenty other kids is no comparison with sharing a bedroom with one or two sisters.

As any parent of more than one child soon learns, children in the same household tend to exhibit the opposite of Philippians 2:3-4: "Do everything from selfishness or empty conceit, and with haughtiness of mind let each of you regard one another as less important than himself; always look out for your own personal interests, and make sure the interests of others never get in your way."

What wonderful opportunity! Within the confines of a home with children, there are more than enough situations daily to teach children the ways of God. The fire of lives intensely lived starts with the sparks generated when, as Proverbs 27:17 says, "Iron sharpens iron, so one man sharpens another."

There are lessons of respect for private property:

Your brother *should* share sometimes, but he *may* deny you access to his electronic keyboard. There are frequent times of accountability: Which preschooler practiced with scissors on sister's language textbook? There are times of reckoning: Brother is punished for pushing sister down because she destroyed his block castle. There is taming of the tongue: The latest school slang for "jerk" must not need to be practiced on defenseless younger siblings. There is appreciation for frugality and the work ethic: "Son, we have committed our extra money to pay for your sister's piano lessons, so you'll have to work to gain the money for your youth group's trip to the mountains." There is training in righteousness: Because Scripture commands denying self, forgiveness, and serving others—even that familiar brother who kicked you and called you an awful name ten minutes ago—there is good reason to help him pick up the million little puzzle pieces from your bedroom floor even though he was the one who made the mess.

Paul wrote to Timothy that "all Scripture is inspired by God and profitable for teaching, for reproof, for correction, for training in righteousness; that the man of God may be adequate, equipped for every good work" (2 Tim. 3:16). This is not just what church members need. This is also what children need: teaching, reproof, correction, training in righteousness, equipping for good works.

These needs draw parents to God and His Word—both to teach from and to gain help in training. In the frighteningly challenging position of teacher and trainer, the parent comes to a new maturity. He or she is forced to dig deep for answers. He is compelled to face again basic issues he may have ignored over the years. Is God real? How do you know? How does God save a person? What does it mean to die to yourself? Where do we go when we're transformed from the kingdom of darkness into the kingdom of light?

This, perhaps, is the most complex aspect of the blessing God sends through children. Their very presence demands so much more than putting food in their mouths. The vulnerability and immense potential of these seedling lives demand acute daily care. The Christian parent who fully embraces the challenges, as well as the sibling who learns to live and love selflessly, reap God's blessings over the long haul.

Scripture says we are made in God's image and that God is a *father*. The more we plumb the depths of parenting, with its endless sacrifices and outpourings of love, the more we come to reflect the One in whose image we are made. The more we love without expecting love in return, the more we appreciate God's unconditional love for us. The more we learn to live sacrificially, the more we become like Christ, the perfect sacrifice.

Selfless, sacrificial lives form strong families. We will see in the next chapter that just as children should bring about maturity and vigor in a family, a growing population also should yield progress and strength in society.

PART 5

THE BIG PICTURE

NINE

GROWING POPULATIONS: THEIR BENEFITS, THEIR ENEMIES

> *In a multitude of people is a king's glory, but in the dearth of people is a prince's ruin.*
>
> Proverbs 14:28

When the Mayflower landed at Plymouth Rock, there were no teeming housing projects, no people waiting in line, no traffic gridlock. The continent was still a pristine wilderness. There were plenty of forests, farmland, and unpolluted water. Sure, there were some people. But the native American Indians represented only one person for every ten square miles.

Hippies and other naturalists have at times glorified the Indians for nobly living at harmony with nature. Yet their life-styles were none too noble by today's standards. The nature they worshipped in various forms proved to be an unkind god.

Those Indians had a life expectancy of about thirty years. They lived in poverty and struggled to feed themselves.[1] They failed to "subdue" the resources under their dominion, as God dictated in Genesis 1:28. They were completely unprepared to defend their land against European invaders. Today they are largely depopulated or assimilated into their conquerors' culture. Their remnants are assigned to reservations, in many cases ravaged by poverty and alcoholism.

Today, every ten square miles of American soil holds not just one person, but more than six hundred people on the average. Even this density is sparse in comparison to many other nations. The entire country is fed by three percent of the population. Life expectancy is seventy-three years. And our standard of living puts much of the world to shame.[2]

God and Growth

Ronald Reagan campaigned for the presidency by asking Americans if they were better off today than they were four years ago. Now I ask: Are you better off today than you would have been as an Indian four hundred years ago? The comparison may seem oversimplified, but then it needs to be. To focus on crowds and shortages of food, housing and wealth, as population control proponents are fond of doing, is to miss the bigger picture. There are problems, which, like the poor, we always have with us. But the overriding tendency of God's creation—from plants to people to populations, provided they are healthy—is toward expansion.

Jesus didn't compare the kingdom of God to a mustard seed because He had a weakness for pastrami on rye. He was talking about growth. The kingdom "is like a mustard seed, which...grows up and becomes larger than all the garden plants" (Mark 4:31-32).

Indeed, all the major Biblical references to growth and fruitfulness—whether discussing growth in the spiritual realm or physical propagation—are upbeat. God never rescinds the Genesis 1:28 mandate to be fruitful and multiply, but repeats it to Noah and the patriarchs. Through Isaiah, God says, "There will be *no end to the increase* of His government or of peace" (Is. 9:7, italics added). Jesus orders the discipling of all nations in the Great Commission (Matt. 28:19).

Warring against God's favor on growth is an elitist effort to control population growth, even to reverse it. Its milder results have been mass movements, funded mainly through the United States, to rob women of their fertility, as we will see in this chapter. Its most hideous expression to date has been the world's greatest genocide, which shows no sign of letting up. It will be discussed in the following chapter.

Rejecting Growth

That an apology has to be made for large families and expanding populations tells a lot about this era. The benefits of growing societies once went unchallenged. No longer.

The belief that the earth is overpopulated reached a frenzy in its modern phase during the 1960s, culminating with the publication of *The Population Bomb*.

The propaganda of the population lobby was so relentless and so completely unchallenged, that the concept of an overpopulated world came to be considered fact, not theory. The hysteria of the 1960s died down, but the legacy lives on. Let there be famine in Ethiopia, poverty in Mexico City, illegitimate births in American high schools, and the population pessimists quickly aver rampant overpopulation.

There are two major problems that the modern overpopulation movement has bequeathed us:

• Though many overpopulation assumptions were unscientific, and though many of the prophecies were wrong, there has been no comparable propaganda campaign to refute the bogus claims.

• Massive population control programs, using millions of our tax dollars, were established and remain in place today. These programs have inflicted incalculable emotional and physical harm on Third World peoples and poor Westerners who never asked for fertility control and don't want it.

The Bible warns that the wisdom of those the world calls wise should automatically be suspect. No truer case of this has come than this century's overpopulation scam. Leading academic, scientific, and political leaders lent their support to the Malthusian theory that population growth would outrun the food supply and other resources. They were wrong. So was Thomas Malthus.

The Population Bomb was the crowning treatise of this era's propaganda. Two years after its publication in 1968, its author, Paul Ehrlich, prophesied that famine would be "directly or indirectly responsible for sixty-five million American deaths in the decade of 1980-89."[3] As writer Tom Bethell points out, little did the forecaster realize that instead the 1980s would become a "decade of best-selling diet books and overweight welfare mamas."[4] Ehrlich's global forecast was even more imminent: Ten million deaths, mostly children, during every year of the 1970s. Nothing close to that came to pass.

Next to *The Population Bomb*, perhaps the biggest overpopulation book scare was *The Limits to Growth*. Its contents reflected the findings of the Club of Rome, a group of thirty international intellectuals assembled in 1968 to grapple with world problems.

The cover of the book's second edition (1974) warns of "imminent global disaster." The back cover entices further:

> Now a team of M.I.T. scientists, with the aid of a giant computer, has completed a study of the future if present growth continues. Their inescapable conclusions are beyond anyone's grimmest fears. *Possibly within as little as seventy years, our social and economic system will collapse unless drastic changes are made very soon* (italics in original).[5]

A blurb from *The National Observer* on the first page says the book "may be as important to mankind as the Council of Nicaea and Martin Luther's Ninety-five Theses."[6]

Pause a minute, though, before you rush out to buy your own copy of this classic to stay up with the New Reformation. For all its impressive growth charts, for all its intricate modeling (with much thanks to the giant computer, no doubt), for its phenomenal sales of four million copies, *Limits* was nothing more than self-justifying hokum.

Julian Simon in *The Ultimate Resource*, his important refutation of overpopulation and vanishing resources, reviews the book's rise and fall:

> *The Limits to Growth* has been blasted as foolishness or fraud by almost every economist who has read it closely and reviewed it in print, for its silly methods as well as for disclosing so little of what the authors did, which makes close inspection impossible.[7]

More incensing, though, is the conclusion to this escapade. Four years after the book's publication—only two years after the second edition trumpeted imminent apocalypse—the Club of Rome changed its mind and decided more growth would be good. Alas, the giant computer was wrong after all. Though this was reported in major media, the recantation had nowhere near the impact of the mammoth public relations campaign that announced the book's findings and accompanied the sale of four million copies.

Yet this is not all. Simon quotes *Time* magazine's account of the reversal, according to the club's founder, Italian industrialist Aurelio Peccei. The book's intention was to jolt people enough to stop ongoing growth trends, Peccei explained, so that international inequities of wealth could be leveled. "In other words, the Club of Rome sponsored and disseminated untruths in an attempt to scare us. Having scared many people with these lies, the club can now tell people the *real* truth" (italics in original).[8]

Was Peccei just trying to save face? Or was it all a preconceived plot? Both explanations are chilling. The first case means the club represented enormous professional talent that reached profoundly stupid conclusions. The second means the club members schemed a deception so morally perverse that its perpetrators deserved, at the very least, to be permanently censured from their fields. As we will see in this chapter and the next, ignorance, deception, and power lust continue to reign unchecked in global population policies sponsored by the United Nations and the United States.

The Myths of Overpopulation

Today's population lobby is a far cry from the early feminists and sexologists fighting for the right to introduce their birth control devices to a staid public. With its millions of dollars and prestigious spokesmen, its henchmen on Ivy League campuses and in glittering United Nations towers around the world, the population lobby is entrenched and credentialed.

In recent decades it has enjoyed a virtual monopoly on the subject of population control. The Roman Catholic hierarchy has been the most visible pro-natalist advocate. Unfortunately, its weapons have been nothing more than tradition, Scripture, and papal authority—certainly of worth to the Christian community, but hardly the thing to influence the icy logic of trigger-happy social scientists.

One notable pro-natalist challenge to emerge was Simon's *The Ultimate Resource* in 1981. He maintained that expanding populations have stimulated economic growth and steadily increased the body of knowledge by which mankind can more efficiently produce goods and manage society. Here are some of the points he argues:

• Population growth is not necessarily constant, inexorable, or (as Malthus argued) geometric. Not only starvation, disease, and war, but economic, political, and social forces determine population levels. Humans do not breed unceasingly to the point of chaos, as do some animals and bugs used in the analogies of the population control boogeymen. Even poor people regulate their own fertility.

• Bigger populations have better chances of producing those rare individuals with special giftings—in science, administration, or other fields—that propel society toward a better standard of living.

• Economies of scale are better in a growing population. "A larger population implies a larger total demand for goods; with larger demand and higher production come division of labor and specialization, larger plants, larger industries, more learning by doing, and other related economies of scale."

• Children are only temporary burdens. They weigh down parents and society approximately for their first twenty-five years, or much less in non-industrial societies. After that, they become blessings. Their productivity as adults helps society progress and outweighs the burdens of their younger years.

• Mineral resources appear to be getting less scarce. The reasoning behind this paradox is that prices—a reflection of supply and demand—have trended down for resources over the long term. This indicates supply (often meaning known reserves) has increased faster than demand, which for most minerals has continued to rise. Additional people increase demand for "the discovery of new deposits, new ways of extracting the resource, and new substitutes for the resource." Atomic energy, for example, would no more have been imaginable even as late as a hundred years ago than would have flight to the moon. Yet that one energy source alone promises long-term electrical generation that significantly reduces the demand on the remaining oil and gas.

• The world's supply of farm land is increasing. Increased productivity has led to larger farms per farmer.

• In more-developed countries, high population growth produces a higher standard of living. The faster-growing countries initially fall behind in per capita income, but they surpass the nations with slower growth in thirty to eighty years.

• Growth can improve living standards. In lesser-developed countries, a moderate rate of population growth "is more likely to lead to a higher standard of living in the long run than either zero population growth or a high rate of population growth."

All this is not to say that growth is without its problems. Growing nations, just like growing families, experience strains. But, as Simon concludes in his book,

> There always will be temporary shortages and resource problems where there are strife, political blundering, and natural calamities— that is, where there are people. But the natural world allows, and the developed world pro-

motes through the marketplace, responses to human needs and shortages in such manner that one backward step leads to 1.0001 steps forward, or thereabouts. That's enough to keep us headed in a life-sustaining direction. The main fuel to speed our progress is our stock of knowledge, and the brake is our lack of imagination. The ultimate resource is people—skilled, spirited, and hopeful people who will exert their wills and imaginations for their own benefit, and so, inevitably, for the benefit of us all.[9]

The Starving Masses

Unfortunately, "responses to human needs and shortages" that take place "through the marketplace" cannot be taken for granted. When governments such as those of Marxist nations try to tinker with the economy, they inevitably thwart the normal ebb and flow of supply and demand that works relatively well to meet needs in a free market economy. A socialist economy removes the incentive to excel in production. After all, if your allotment of money or grain is fixed, why break your neck at work?

Only in recent years has China introduced a measured amount of state-sanctioned capitalism to inject some life into its stagnant economy. The results have been fantastic. But so far, there has been too much adherence to communism to allow the economy to break forth in such a way that the nation's working population will become economic blessings instead of the economic burdens that the state's economic planners see them to be.

Or consider Ethiopia, where the masses were starving following a drastic reduction in population. The famine of the early 1980s that gave us the *We Are the World* guilt video was generally attributed to drought, not overpopulation. Yet the widely publicized images of starving, ill-clad Africans with toothpick arms, bloated bellies, and fly-covered faces subtly reinforced years of overpopulation propaganda that used the same kind of shock-logic. After all, food would go a lot farther if there were fewer people to share it, right?

Less publicized than the drought were the policies of Marxist dictator Mengistu Haile-Mariam. As many as one million people were killed or reported missing between 1974, the date of Ethiopia's communist revolution, and 1982. More than two million people fled the country.

Mengistu seized church property. He drafted young farmers into the military. He collectivized the farms. The state denied seed, fertilizer, and fair prices to farmers after state farms and forced cooperatives were formed. Farmers who continued to save food for famine, as they had learned to from experience, were guilty of the capitalist crime of "hoarding." Many paid for their crime in mass executions.

Mengistu lured residents out of northern areas, where there was civil war, with promises of Western aid. He resettled them in the south, where they joined other starving Ethiopians. Meanwhile, the aid was delayed, misused, or denied for political and military purposes.[10]

Government corruption, collectivization, violation of freedoms, anarchy, civil war—these are too often the culprits behind the poverty that fertility controllers like to blame on overpopulation.

Of course, to the neo-Malthusian, no amount of development or prosperity that emanates from free markets, with or without growing populations, is evidence of good things to come. Now, they say, things are different (though this has been the argument of enlightened pessimists throughout the ages).

By Malthusian reasoning, the more densely populated countries should be poorer. But there is no such correlation. Consider five countries and their densities: United States, 65 people per square mile; China, 285; India, 583; Japan, 826; and Taiwan, 1,401.[11]

The United States and Japan are world economic leaders, and Taiwan is showing remarkable economic strength for a small island. Overpopulation logic would lead us to assume that these productive nations are low-density countries. Yet with densities as different as 65, 826, and 1,401 people per square mile, it's obvious that how tightly their workers are squeezed together has very little to do with their happiness and success.

By the same token, population figures would also indicate that India and China, with much more breathing room for their citizens than Japan and Taiwan, would enjoy a higher level of prosperity. After all, land and other resources would be divided among fewer people. Such is not the case. Economic problems in China and India have set the stage for the most aggressive fertility control programs in recent decades.

Clearly, then, high population density is not *by itself* a cause of poverty.

War on the Womb

Thorough refutations, such as *The Ultimate Resource,* have not been able to counteract the inroads made by those who espouse the view that the world is overpopulated. The first legacy, then, of the population lobby, has been ideology. The movement has successfully instilled the idea of overpopulation as a present fact and growing threat. Those who want to argue from a premise of overpopulation—whether the subject be poverty or condom handouts at high schools—need not bother to defend it as a theory.

The second and most tangible legacy of the modern population lobby is the global campaign to reduce births. Millions of U.S. tax dollars are funneled through public and private channels to keep Americans and certain foreign peoples from reproducing as much as they normally would. Thanks to well-meaning contributors to private foundations and misinformed or apathetic taxpayers, the United States has been a major partner in spreading unwanted contraception and sterilization throughout the world.

The U.S. Agency for International Development (AID) is one of the most active parties in population control. In 1965, its population planning programs, funded by tax money, totaled two million dollars. By 1985, they had grown to $250 million. Along with AID are groups such as the Rockefeller Foundation, the Population Council, the Population Crisis Committee, the International Planned Parenthood Federation, the UN Fund for Population Activities, the Ford Foundation, Zero Population Growth,

Negative Population Growth, National Organization for Non-Parents, Population Services International, Pathfinder Fund, and the Association for Voluntary Sterilization.

AID is the godfather in this group. It funnels tax dollars directly to birth control recipients or through some of the other groups listed. From 1969 through at least 1977, AID's population control spending well exceeded its total spending for other health programs.[12] You would think AID was fighting AIDS or some other fatal plague, but it was serving no higher cause than the perceived need to keep wombs barren.

What has all this money been buying?

Thanks, But No Thanks

Americans have long been accused of ethnocentrism, that is, thinking their culture to be the dominant and only proper one. We think that because we regard sex primarily for pleasure and bonding, foreigners should, too. Because we regard certain conceptions as unwanted accidents, everyone else should. Because we treat pregnancy as an extra feature we order at our discretion, like power steering on a new car, everyone else should. Because we think smaller families always translate into more prosperous living, we believe foreigners reason that way, too.

Sorry, but they don't all think American.

Good old American ethnocentrism has gone on a drunken joy ride around the world in the area of fertility planning. Unfortunately, there's nothing joyous about the physical and emotional carnage we're leaving.

First, much of the world, especially Third World nations, shares the Hebrew esteem for fertility, even though the people are not Jews.

Author Germaine Greer tells the story of a "well baby parade" in a village health facility in India. A pregnant woman with a withered arm and a limp, due to polio, appeared in line. She carried a son with her good arm. Ms. Greer prompted the doctor to suggest the woman accept birth control after the baby's birth. The surprised woman replied that would not be necessary.

> "My sisters-in-law help me and we have land." She hoisted her healthy child up a little higher on her arm and smiled upon us like a queen. He was her victory over disability. Only he could annihilate all the suffering and the weariness of her struggle to live with only one good arm and one good leg. She had won, because she had become that most auspicious of women, the fruitful wife.[13]

For Americans to laugh this off as the outdated notions of a backward people who have yet to progress into modern life is a self-indictment. We are the foolish ones—so unappreciative of family, so unaware of historical primacy of procreation, so easily seduced by the modern gloss put on barrenness.

Another reason why many non-Americans don't share our enthusiasm over fertility control is because of what they see in us. Most of the subjects of intense fertility control efforts are small nations. All of them are poor. They may bad-mouth Yankee imperialists, but in two respects they want to emulate us: They want to be wealthy, and they want to be big and strong.

Some of these people see the Agency for International Development experts for the meddling outsiders that they are. These nations' rulers, contemplating attractive foreign aid tied to population control projects, have not always seen as clearly.

The Quiet War

America's war on fertility has been one of the most devious anti-natalist campaigns ever waged. First, it is well-funded. The U.S. contributions to foreign population control since 1965 have exceeded the combined total of all other countries.[14] Second, from a domestic standpoint, this campaign that equates procreation with social burden has been downright secretive at times.

Jacqueline Kasun, in her marvelous exposé of the population control movement, *War Against Population*, described the clandestine nature of those who wish to impose the warped ideas of American population controllers on various nations:

> Early in the 1970s the United States' foreign aid bureaucracy spelled out its plan to bring world population growth to a halt. In a classified document prepared in 1974 and not declassified until 1980, the aid planners voiced their intent to bring about "a two-child family on the average" throughout the world by the year 2000.[15]

The plan also named the countries where efforts should be concentrated: India, Bangladesh, Pakistan, Ethiopia, Mexico, Indonesia, Brazil, the Philippines, Thailand, Egypt, Turkey, Nigeria, and Colombia.

To add muscle to their plan, AID officials persuaded Congress in 1978 to pass a law that linked various types of aid to countries' commitment to population control programs. In other words, the population cabal had legal rein for international blackmail. By virtue of American largesse in foreign aid, they could induce foreign leaders into accepting anti-natalist propaganda programs, followed by vasectomies, sterilizations, and such, to which the populace, from the experience of recent decades, had already shown an aversion.[16]

Some of the population control zealots at times were not so secretive. The director of AID's Office of Population, Reimert T. Ravenholt, demanded in a 1977 newspaper interview "the sterilization of one-quarter of the fertile women of the world to meet U.S. goals of population control...."[17] Similar fervor came from Robert S. McNamara, as executive director of the World Bank, which funnels a large portion of American aid to foreign countries. In a 1977 interview, he said that the failure of population control measures in some nations could drive those countries "to more coercive methods."[18] Or, as both AID and the National Security Council said in separate documents, family planning services and education alone may not be enough to reduce birth rates to two (or slightly more) children per woman.[19]

The Victims

They were right. Those measures alone were not enough. Consequently, various disincentives and incentives have been tried. Ms. Kasun notes that a favorite method is the "village system." This combines strategies that put pressure on individuals by rewarding or punishing the group, or village.

For instance, during a program in Indonesia, the monthly village meeting would begin with a roll call where each man would say whether he and the Missus were using contraceptives. Replies would be plotted on a prominently displayed village map. Local field workers who would recruit new candidates for birth control would receive a bonus. The government—always the source of blessings in the humanist mentality that likes to play God by controlling creation—would bestow increased food supplements, health services, and other rewards to villages that met their targets for contraceptive practice.[20]

In Taiwan, families have been awarded bank deposits, redeemable for education, when they have only two or three children.[21] "An AID-financed sterilization drive in El Salvador was reported as using a quota system to achieve more than 20,000 sterilizations a year without adequate provisions for voluntary consent."[22] In Bangladesh, another AID-financed program reportedly offered direct payments to those who recruited sterilization candidates, as well as to the patients themselves, some of whom reportedly did not understand the nature of the operation.[23]

In Singapore, the government played hardball. Though some of these controls have since been reversed, the government for a time charged higher hospital delivery fees for each additional child, abolished paid maternity leave, abolished the priority for large families in the allocation of subsidized housing, and abolished the income tax relief for the fourth child and subsequent children in a family.[24]

Thailand was reluctant at first, but came to be considered a model client of family planning aid. After the Thai government accepted a $3.5 million AID program in 1968, the World Bank chipped in with more than $700 million in loans during 1969-1977, and the United States upped its ante to Thailand's economic and military assistance.[25] As part of this turnaround, Thailand had initiated an innovative maternity ward program. Thai mothers had the pleasure of getting, along with information about newborn care, a hospital staff hard-sell for sterilization so that their new baby will be their last baby. One hospital reported forty-three percent of its obstetrical patients were sterilized.[26]

The favorite source of laboratory specimens for the population lobby's experiments has been India. The world's second most populous nation, it trailed China's one billion people with about 740 million in the mid-1980s.

Some of the earliest birth control efforts in India, which took place in the 1950s, failed or were of little consequence. By the 1960s the nation was seeing still-climbing birth rates in spite of increased spending and an army of seventy thousand full-time birth control workers. Consequently, the pace was stepped up in the early 1970s with mass sterilizations.

Thousands of vasectomies were performed, following tremendous public relations and education efforts. As in the past, it was largely older men who signed up. The marginal costs to reach younger candidates, with more years of paternity ahead, were higher.

The government then became more coercive in its methods. Road paving, connection to the electrical system, and other favors which the state could control became part of political bartering. You want cooperation from Uncle Mahatma? You get a vasectomy to help the bureaucrats meet their district quota. And the operations were performed with less than guaranteed safety. One district had a fourth of the men reporting adverse effects to the operation.[27]

All of this paled, however, in the frenzy of 1975-77. A goal of 1.5 million sterilizations was decreed; 837,000 were performed, some of them forcibly on men picked up in raids. There were 1,774 deaths as a result of the operation, and untold numbers who suffered and continue to suffer from it.[28]

All along, the idea was that the bureaucrats and foreign intelligentsia knew better than the common people. Ms. Greer observes:

> It takes the refined brutality of Western aid to shove expensive contraceptive technology into a village whose people would feel a good deal better and produce more food and get more done generally, if a few pence were spent on eradicating the parasites which infest them.[29]

Sterilization has also made its mark in the United States, though more selectively. "The pattern of who is sterilized is slanted systematically toward the poor and those on welfare," maintains Thomas Shapiro in his book *Population Control Politics*.[30] He documents many cases in this country that exemplify the same deceptions that have been foisted on other peoples: concealing from the patient the full implications of sterilization, for example, or bureaucrats rashly deciding to sterilize candidates they deem unable to regulate their own fertility or unfit to be parents.

In more recent years, at least from the White House, the population control movement has been challenged. The Reagan administration, at the 1984 International Conference on Population in Mexico City, declared population growth is "of itself a neutral phenomenon." It further said the true cause of poverty was "governmental control of economies, a development which effectively constrained economic growth." The U.S. delegation condemned abortion, involuntary sterilization, and other coercive birth control measures. It said the United States would withdraw support from organizations that promote abortion as a means of family planning.[31] In 1986 and 1987, the administration redirected to other population agencies the annual $25 million grant for the UN Fund for Population Activities because the UN fund had supported China's coercive birth control program.[32] President Bush continued the Reagan administration's anti-abortion stance on several fronts. But as the twelve-year Republican occupation of the White House ended in 1992, it appeared such policies could be reversed.

Though Reagan and Bush were willing to confront the abortion lobby, they did little to reverse the scope or vigor of the population control bureaucracy. The sad truth is that not only is the United States guilty in tolerating abortion inside its own borders, but it is guilty of directly or indirectly encouraging it in other nations. Those in positions of influence have also funded and verbally endorsed violations of personal freedoms through deceptive sterilization and coercive contraception.

An elite clique perpetuates these policies. They are using our tax dollars, with no mandate from the taxpayers, to crush the fertility of people around the globe, most of whom know perfectly well how to regulate their family size. It is an unconscionable establishment of the-child-as-burden mentality. It wars against Scripture's value system.

The Exodus Explosion

Population controllers, for all their behind-the-scenes activities, have been quite public when it suits their purposes. For example, they have grafted into our language some clever terminology, such as "child-free." This is the happy-talk version of the more dismal "childless."

Another term is "population explosion," describing the Malthusian nightmare that was supposed to burst forth in this century. Yet what may have been history's first population boom is recorded in the Bible after Jacob and his clan migrated to Egypt. In 430 years, while their descendants apparently intermarried with Egyptians and had plenty of babies, they multiplied to perhaps two million people.

The Hebrews left Egypt with Egyptian plunder, but they were otherwise impoverished by our standards—homeless, jobless, and dependent on God's daily provision for food and water. By mid-twentieth century logic, these swarming masses would have been people well qualified for a shipload of AID-financed condoms and a hefty World Bank loan.

By God's perspective, they had not multiplied enough. He promised to drive the pagans gradually from Canaan "until you become fruitful" (Ex. 23:30). As author Gary North notes, their fruitfulness—of people, herds, etc.—was tied to covenantal faithfulness, as indicated in Exodus 23:25-26:[33]

> "But you shall serve the Lord your God, and He will bless your bread and your water; and I will remove sickness from your midst. There shall be no one miscarrying or barren in your land; I will fulfill the number of your days."

North concludes, "There is no indication in the revelation of God to His Old Covenant people that they would experience anything except large families, zero miscarriages, and high rates of population growth, *if* they would conform themselves to His law" (italics in original).[34]

The Israelites, of course, failed the test. They worshipped idols, sacrificed children, and continually rebelled. They rejected the promise of population growth and godly rule, so God ejected them from the promised land.

Growing numbers of people remain a part of God's plan, but growth alone is not His ultimate goal. He is after a contrite heart and obedience. Fruitfulness will follow. The state's humanistic attempt to stem or reduce populations will not bring prosperity, just as mindless breeding by nominal Christians will not cause God's blessing to rain down.

The covenant-keeping community and a nation of such communities should expect and welcome burgeoning populations. At the same time, they must also resist the politicians and social planners who war against fertility. As the next chapter will show, when those in power tremble over the people multiplying in their land, as Pharaoh did with the Hebrews, trouble is at hand.

TEN

CHINA'S SELF-INFLICTED GENOCIDE

> *Then Pharaoh commanded all his peo-*
> *ple, saying, "Every son who is born*
> *you are to cast into the Nile, and every*
> *daughter you are to keep alive."*
>
> Exodus 1:22

Eighteen village women, their bellies round with child, sit on plank benches. Their eyes are red from crying and lack of sleep.

"You must realize that none of you has any choice in this matter," says the party official. "Your pregnancy affects everyone in the commune, indeed everyone in the country. You will be given a shot which will cause you to abort. If necessary, the fetus will be removed by cesarean."[1]

> A woman is in labor. A bucket of water sits near the bed. She and her husband eagerly await the moment when the wiggly child will emerge. Will it be a boy?

No. The newborn girl's taste of life outside
the womb is short. She receives a baptism of
death in a nearby pail of water. Her crime:
being born a girl in the People's Republic of
China.[2]

Every May, Israel and various communities around
the world conduct *yom hashoah* (day of destruction)
memorials for the Jews killed in the Nazi Holocaust.
The slogan "Never again" provides a constructive
focal point for the otherwise morbid recollections.
All sensible heads nod in agreement: Never again
must the world stand by as state machinery performs
genocide.

The pro-life community has long recognized the
hollowness of "never again." In the United States, the
abortion holocaust continues at 1.6 million deaths a
year, more than twenty-five million since the 1973
legalization of abortion.

What has been far less publicized here is the highly
advanced state-sponsored genocide in China. Under a
national policy that limits families to one child, the
state coerces contraception, sterilization, abortion,
and infanticide. Of an estimated fifty-three million
abortions performed between 1980 and 1985, an estimated ninety percent were involuntary.[3] What China
has accomplished is nothing less than "the world's
first national compulsory family planning program."[4]

The frightening thing is not just that China has a
bigger abortion problem than the United States. After
all, the natal death movement there is much different.
There is no National Organization of Women lobbying the ruling class to endorse abortion as a woman's

right to her body. There is no sprawling welfare class generating illegitimate babies and thereby prompting do-gooders to stem the tide of supposedly unwanted lives.

In spite of the differences, there's one ominous similarity: The driving force behind China's lethal population program is fear of population growth—a phobia well-instilled in America. In other words, it *can* happen here.

A documentary on the Public Broadcasting System's *Nova* show, aired in 1984, implied just that. After a one-hour whitewash on China's one-child policy, the narrator abruptly asked how the United States would cope with its own alleged overpopulation. PBS had it neatly figured out: mass education, then limiting births, and finally assuring that all government rules are applied equally—just as the Chinese were doing.

"Voluntary," Chinese Style

If you were to call up Beijing and ask why they are forcing women to get abortions, the officials would say there must be some mistake. All the abortions and sterilizations performed there are voluntary. The comrades are perfectly willing to make sacrifices for the betterment of their state, the bureaucrats would say. After all, with more than one billion people— one-fifth of the world's population—China has too many people.

The eighteen pregnant village women, for example, were given a "voluntary" choice. They could have an abortion, or they could stay incarcerated in the room.

Should they choose to stay in the room and stick it out, they would be taken to the commune clinic, the party official said. And, reading from the population control regulations, he said, "The safety of over-quota children born in the commune clinic is not guaranteed." Hence, a simplified choice: abortion now or infanticide later.[5]

At one point the program did have a semblance of voluntariness. However, a strong set of incentives and disincentives, economic and otherwise, made it prudent for families to stop at one child. This period was from the time the one-child policy was announced, in 1979, until about 1982. By then, in most areas, a family was not allowed to conceive a second or higher-order child.[6]

If such a pregnancy developed and the mother managed to escape or endure the advance harassment to abort, she would still have to produce, upon her arrival at the clinic, a state-issued certificate allowing the birth. Otherwise involuntary abortion or infanticide would likely follow.

Steven Mosher, as a Stanford University graduate student, observed many aspects of the Chinese program firsthand. He later made headlines as he exposed what he saw. This angered the academic community, which was more interested in maintaining a peaceful exchange with China, and he was kicked out of the graduate program. He writes that in the area where he was,

> the child is killed by means of the "poison shot" into the womb or by strangling as it emerges. Michael Weisskopf of the

Washington Post found that in one area of North China the usual method appears to be an injection of formaldehyde into the soft spot in the infant's head, or the actual crushing of its skull by forceps.[7]

A *New York Times* reporter wrote of roundups of thousands of Chinese women who were forced to have abortions. He also

described women "locked in detention cells or hauled before mass rallies and harangued into consenting to abortions." He told of "vigilantes [who] abducted pregnant women on the streets and hauled them off, sometimes handcuffed or trussed, to abortion clinics," and of "aborted babies which were...crying when they were born."[8]

Some couples, especially those who live in or escape to the back country, manage to get away with a second birth. But the state does not turn its back. The parents usually face curtailment of privileges, such as lower wages, less farm land, or restricted educational opportunities for their children. By the same token, those couples who clearly get with the program, such as by submitting to sterilization, supposedly get rewarded. The government heaps praise upon entire factories and villages that demonstrate exemplary fertility rates. Rewards, however, have diminished as such a large segment of the population have now signed the one-child pledge.

Where Have All the Girls Gone?

When government starts tinkering with matters out-side of basic governance, you can expect problems. When price controls are set, the limits spread like cancer through the intricate network of supply and demand, creating shortages, unwanted surpluses, and illegal trade. Limiting fertility—essentially another form of economic control—makes things, in a similar fashion, go haywire. Only it's worse.

China's one-child policy will yield devastating results in several ways. Children will grow up without the joyful (and otherwise) learning experiences of having brothers and sisters. In coming generations, there will be no uncles, aunts, cousins, brothers-in-law or sisters-in-law. In one master stroke, the state has excised huge chunks of rich, normal family relationships. This is tragic enough, but there are more serious problems already at hand.

The Chinese, more than most people in industrialized nations, value boys more than girls. There is a good reason. Upon marriage, a girl fully joins the family of her husband. In later years, she and her husband are expected to care for his aging parents, not hers. So it's in a couple's best interest to have as many sons as possible. Elderly Chinese without sons, especially those in rural areas, face bleak sunset years: As their health fails, they are relegated to lower-paying agricultural jobs, scarcely able to support themselves.

This explains the bedside bucket of water. Allowed only one child, parents are willing to murder in hopes their luck will improve with another conception.

Other reports have spoken of baby girls' bodies float-ing in a Shanghai river. On the surface, China does not officially acknowledge this embarrassing problem with female infanticide, but figures have leaked out. A census revealed that by 1981—only about two years into the one-child program—the birth ratio was 108.5 males to every 100 females. This means China was producing more boys than would be expected under the international norm of 1.06 boys for every 100 girls.[9] Mosher estimated 1.3 million deaths from female infanticide in China by 1985.[10]

In the field, the low-level and mid-level hacks devoted to meeting population quotas have no prob-lem with their neighbors killing baby girls. No means is too immoral to satisfy the drive to suppress popula-tion.

Infanticide is abhorrent on its face. There is neither an excuse for a state policy that precipitates it, nor is there an excuse for private citizens to practice it. But even if you put aside the immorality of the situation, the practical problems from this national crime will be felt for years in China.

Ten years from now, there will not be enough brides to go around. Homosexuality, rape, and the typical violent crimes committed by unsettled young men are likely to increase.

The acceptance of gender-selective murder has also spread to other Asian countries that favor male babies. Sex-test centers have proliferated in India, often near abortion mills that will perform an abor-tion for as little as seven dollars. Sex-testing has also become popular in South Korea. Seven hospitals there have reported that more boys than girls are being born, whereas the opposite had been true before.[11]

The social problems that stem from having abnormal ratios of men and women will be bad enough. But there are more serious demographic imbalances that will cause even greater problems than what China's population planners feared from population growth.

Too Many Old Folks

You don't need a demographic computer model to figure that if every two adults have only one child, there will soon be more and more elderly people and few young people. This is Communist China's future. It is no workers' paradise.

The ranks of the elderly will swell, yet the state has virtually deprived them of their traditional and best source of care. Only about half of the elderly will have a son's family—and only one such unit—to provide any housing and support in the final years. It will be an accelerated version of the problem the United States has with Social Security—not enough workers to support an increasing number of retirees.

Hitler's "final solution" encompassed the "useless eaters"—the retarded, the handicapped and others—who did not fit the state-defined master race. It is difficult to imagine that China will have any choice but to reach a similar solution for its useless elderly when they begin to take up a disproportionate amount of the population. Mosher opines:

> They would be sent to study sessions where they would be told that, "for the sake of the

modernization program, they should 'voluntarily' submit to euthanasia." To wear down their resistance and that of their families, economic incentives would be offered, such as better housing for their son and daughter-in-law, an education for their grandchild, and a cash bonus to be awarded after the act had been committed. Sanctions would also be imposed, such as fines for each month they refuse to terminate their existence, or perhaps a reduction in the size of the fields leased to their family by the state.[12]

Such conjecture is not paranoia, Mosher points out. The methods are already in full swing at the cradle end of the Chinese life cycle.

This is not a problem that the Communist Chinese can suddenly wake up to in 2001 and try to correct with a policy shift. The damage will have been done. No party can by fiat resurrect hundreds of millions of workers whose lives were snuffed out before birth or shortly after. The creation of life is God's business. That's why interference with it brings chaos and, ultimately, God's judgment. Man cannot treat God's blessing as curse and expect to escape consequences.

Finally, there is the question of economics. For the Chinese planners, it is the only question. Will lower growth mean a more prosperous country? Will there be more per capita income, more resources to divide, more modernization?

No. What is true in the spiritual realm is true in the natural—children are a blessing, particularly when they reach adulthood and produce more than they consume. Proverbs 26:27 says of the evil man, "He who digs a pit will fall into it." The Chinese are digging an economic grave for their living with the graves of their dead infants. The broader principles of growth and progress, as explained in the last chapter, show that soon enough the vanity of the Chinese effort will become painfully clear. No economic system—communism or capitalism—can thrive, or even survive, when its working class dwindles in proportion to its elderly. Furthermore, the spiritual and emotional health of a people, Christian or otherwise, will not long endure an overlord that crushes normal family expansion.

I wish I could say that the United States is as fervently pro-natalist as the Chinese government is anti-natalist, but such is not the case. The musings of public television regarding a coming time of fertility curtailment here are hardly idle. As chapter 9 showed, our foreign aid bureaucracy drafted a plan in the 1970s—and kept it classified for six years—that called for the two-child family to become a world-wide norm by the year 2000. This included reaching a "near stability" level (meaning close to a 2.1 total fertility rate) for the United States.[13]

The World Bank, heavily funded by the United States, in 1984 endorsed the population control incentives and disincentives that existed in more than thirty countries. The report described the Chinese program in detail. Other members of the population control hierarchy have spoken in glowing terms of the Chinese effort.[14]

America's own Agency for International Development, in fact, indirectly supported the Chinese program by contributing to the International Planned

Parenthood Federation and the UN Fund for Population Activities. Both of these groups gave money to the Chinese program.[15]

The "good" news in all of this, if you can call it that, is that the U.S. government may never need to start its own coercive birth control program. After all, our fertility rate, at 1.8 to 2.0 in recent years, is already below replacement. One reason the government is not presently tempted to draft a fertility storm trooper squad is that its domestic policies have quietly helped to lower birth rates in recent decades. The next chapter will look at what those developments are and how they threaten the moral and economic future of our nation. More than following those strange Oriental communists, we have indirectly chosen to emulate a laid-back country that is more our style—Sweden, the Scandinavian paradise of sex and socialism.

ELEVEN

SWEDEN: AMERICA'S FORERUNNER?

> *Can a throne of destruction be allied*
> *with Thee, one which devises mischief*
> *by decree? They band themselves*
> *together against the life of the right-*
> *eous, and condemn the innocent to*
> *death.*
>
> Psalm 94:20-21

"I have seen the future and it works," said Lincoln Steffans, the turn-of-the-century muckraker who had visited Moscow.

Some malcontents in this country continue to see the future through Marxist-tinted glasses. America is flawed, they say, with its voracious capitalists, its patriarchal families that greedily own and bequeath personal property, its remnant of oppressed mothers who bother to care for their own children.

The Soviet Union, however, became more and more difficult to champion. Its future, contrary to Steffans, did not work. The relentless barbarism and violation of human rights at the hands of the Soviet leaders made it awkward to defend for all but the numbest liberal sensitivities. Finally, at the end of the 1980s, the whole wretched experiment crumbled.

Ah, but then there is Sweden. Its state-run day care and other progressive social experiments, heavily driven by government, fill the Christmas wish list of American liberals. For example, Coretta Scott King, the widow of slain civil rights leader Martin Luther King, suggests in her syndicated column that Americans become educated about "the world's most socially innovative democracy." And don't muss the vision of this latest Utopia with any facts, she pleads: "Unable to produce any hard evidence of social decay or political repression in Sweden, (conservatives) have been reduced to parroting inaccurate cliches about suicide rates and oppressive taxes."[1]

I don't know how hard evidence has to be for Mrs. King to consider it more than "inaccurate cliches." And I don't know why she thinks extremely high rates of taxation and suicide bear no relevance to that society's health. Exhibits A-Z are in on the Swedish case, and there are no smiles on the jury's faces. The evidence is "hard" enough and sharp enough to cut diamonds. There has been some turnaround in Sweden's social disintegration in the early 1990s, as we will see. But the responsibility for us non-Swedes is to see what this "most socially innovative democracy" has led to.

Dismantling the Family

Babies are not the rage in Sweden. The nation's total fertility rate in the mid-1980s was 1.7. This was only slightly below the U.S. rate at that time of 1.8, but well below the 2.1 replacement level, and one of the lowest levels in the world.

Swedes, however, do boast of other demographic distinctions that are second to none: During the 1980s, Sweden's marriage rate fell to the lowest level in the industrial world; the cohabitation rate reached the highest rate in the industrialized world; and the divorce rate may have led the industrialized world.[2]

This is of only minor significance to the secular observer, for whom there is little difference between cohabitation and marriage, and for whom divorce is a right, not a tragedy. From God's vantage point of family, there is a major distinction. Not only is family considered a covenantal institution, but its normative form is to bear fruit in the form of children. Sweden's rejection of marriage simultaneously rejects the blessing of children.

It comes as no surprise to the Christian observer that cohabitation, as a sinful life-style outside of God's authority, is deceptively disappointing. The Scandinavian "free love" image of promiscuous, blonde, Nordic beauties is great for selling men's magazines. It is not so good for social stability. Consider, first, "Swedish divorce rates are nearly eighty percent higher among couples who cohabit before marriage than among those who do not."[3] Second, fertility among cohabiting couples is half that of married couples.[4]

Ironically, feminists typically join forces with social liberals in endorsing societies such as modern-day Sweden. Yet the "hard evidence" Mrs. King can't seem to find shows that women are the losers. With marriage rates extremely low and no moral or social bonds to make cohabitation a lifelong commitment, women face lengthening odds that their lives after age thirty-five—when their sexual prime is past—will be lived without a mate. And the declining birth rate raises the odds that they also will trudge through their elderly years without the emotional or financial support of children or grandchildren.

This is no happenstance development. The Swedish people, with the support of their government, have pursued an aggressively anti-family structure for their society. The state now functions as a quasi-family agent. It is doing a lousy job. But the people allow it.

The rise of Swedish statism is a relatively new phenomenon. Because its early stages have been so similar to the progressive demands on this side of the ocean and directly affect fertility and child raising, it is worth tracing its development. Pray that it is not a preview of America's political agenda as this century concludes.

Good Intentions, Bad Results

Much of Sweden's social climate today is rooted in the battle to level gender distinctions. As in America, when there is a war over sex roles, motherhood is the first casualty.

Carlson, of the Rockford Institute on the Family in America, records how Sweden's Parliamentary Committee on Women's Work, in a 1938 report, said women have a right to be paid workers regardless of marital or parental status. Working outside the home was necessary and inevitable for women, it said. The committee recommended expanding the number of day care centers. It also called for what American liberals now call "comparable wage," meaning women should always earn as much as men.[5]

These ideas would see their day, but for the time being they gestated. The nation enjoyed the tranquil domesticity that America and other Western nations enjoyed after World War II.

Then, in the 1960s, the sex role debate resurfaced with greater support. Carlson notes that school officials, for example, decided to vigorously counteract traditional views of male and female roles presented to students. The comparable wage became a mandate. The "working family," in which both partners would labor outside the home and children would be cared for in centers, became the goal. As it turned out, not only would women have the opportunity to work, but thanks to an altered tax structure, they would have no choice but to work in order for their family to enjoy a normal living standard.

The tax law was changed to remove, in effect, the joint return for a married couple, and with it the protection afforded a one-income family. "Moreover, marginal Swedish income taxes were increased in the period (such rates now approach 100 percent at even a modest income level), making extra personal effort to support a family on one income virtually impossible," writes Carlson.[6]

Pushing women into the work force quite naturally discouraged childbearing. Even if a Swedish family decided to care for a child at home and refused to partake of the lavish spread of government services—day care, free children's meals, free diapers, for example—it penalized itself because it already had paid for these services through exorbitant taxes.

The pressure worked. Influential Swedish economists Alva and Gunnar Myrdal expressed the tenor of the times by describing the traditional family system as "almost...pathological." The proportion of working women with preschool children rose from twenty-seven percent to sixty-four percent between 1965 and 1980. Carlson noted other reports indicating that virtually all mothers of infants were working by the late 1980s.[7]

Writing in 1992, Carlson observed some signs that the pendulum had begun to swing the other way in Sweden.[8] From 1983 to 1990, the number of live births increased 35 percent, due at least in part to a generous parental leave program. A change in law in 1988 brought many cohabiting couples to a point of commitment and caused the marriage rate to more than double in one year. During 1991 elections, the three parties that fared best at the polls were those that emphasized traditional family values.

Nevertheless, the Swedish welfare machine is far from being dismantled; it will take more than a spurt in birth and marriage rates to effect substantive change in typical families. Perhaps such transition is indeed in the works, just as Sweden's East European neighbors seem committed to forsaking their socialist past.

Without such change, Sweden and its families would have a bleak future. Under the system that has prevailed in recent decades, the only party to whom children are a blessing is the state. A continual stream of children into day care centers further establishes statist power; it reinforces to young women that, yes, this is the normal way of life for the Modern Family, and, golly, it sure is easier to punch a computer keyboard than to spoon baby food into a screaming mouth.

Of course, the less publicized truth is that children are also a blessing, a vanishing species of blessing, to the Swedish state and every other nation that needs workers to fuel a welfare state, and especially a state-funded pension system. The Myrdals, themselves architects of the Swedish welfare system, warned both their nation and ours in the early 1940s that Social Security doesn't compute. Families have always cared for their own elderly, so it made good sense—not at first, but later—to have many children and grandchildren. But if you shift old-age care to a government-controlled system funded by everybody, there is no incentive to have children. Why not let everybody else's kids pay for your retirement?

The United States: Play Now, Pay Later

Indeed, shrewd Americans have figured out that they can exploit the same basic weakness in the Social Security system. It's like the rationale used in cheating the phone company or the Internal Revenue Service: They're so big they won't miss my payment. Only in this case, the cheating takes the form of producing future wage-earners, also known as babies. The way our system is structured, it makes no difference whether you produce ten strapping workers to help fund the retirement plan or whether you stay childless. Your payout at retirement will be the same.

Social Security, conceived in the 1930s, needed only a maximum annual contribution of thirty dollars per worker in 1947. By 1965, the top figure was $174—still low, considering cost-of-living increases by that time. Social Security taxes rose during the 1970s and

1980s, and by 1993, the maximum amount was $4,406 on the worker, plus an equal match by the employer.

That rising tax rate mirrors the erosion of the system's revenue base. In the late 1940s, there were 13 workers generating taxes for every retiree. By 1988, there were 3.8 workers for every retiree. The Social Security Administration forecasts that by 2035, there will be only 2.5 workers for every retiree. Demographer Ben Wattenberg estimates the 2035 figure at a flat 2.0.[9] So by the hundredth anniversary of the Social Security system, the ratio of producers to retirees will be, a small fraction of what it was in the 1940s.

Of course, before the balance tips that severely, there will have to be changes: higher taxes, decreased or delayed benefits, or both. Not a pretty picture for those of us still with many years in the work force. Nor for our children.

As bad as that is, the end is not in sight. As Wattenberg has detailed, America is now enjoying the lull before the storm in its fertility path. A massive number of Baby Boom girls are now mothers bearing a quantitatively large, but proportionately small, number of babies. Remember, this is no brief aberration. Our birth rate has been below replacement level since 1972.

As the effect of that low rate kicks in over the next several decades, population levels will plunge and the median age will rise. The smaller young and middle-aged cohort will be supporting a huge elderly population, living even longer, thanks to medical advances. And unless a widespread reversal of private attitudes has taken place, the crisis will continue. Those in their thirties, forties and fifties not only will face an unmanageable burden of comprehensive care for millions of elderly who demand their Social Security payout and who have few, if any, children to rely upon, but those middle-aged workers also will find little potential for new revenues from their children, a dwindling cohort of overtaxed workers.

Looking strictly at the broad economic picture, it is equally bleak. The factor taken for granted in America's two centuries of economic development and strength has been continual growth. Population (markets) were always getting bigger. Entrepreneurial risk was always cushioned as long as the economy was growing. If demand for one product expired, demand for two other products and a new service took its place. Look at today's jobs—automobile line worker, stockbroker, computer programmer, appliance repairman. Many did not exist even a hundred years ago. When population growth is stagnant, and most certainly when it declines, it undermines the entire economy. Housing, cars, food—you name it, it will suffer directly or indirectly when markets contract. And Social Security revenues will shrivel even faster when the economy it taxes is contracting.

Part of this problem is the system's self-destructive nature. As the Myrdals pointed out, a state-funded retirement removes the long-term incentive for having children. So there are fewer births. But the system is structured essentially like a chain letter, a pyramid scheme, premised on an ever-larger base—in this case a growing population—funneling goods to the top. When the chain letter gets tossed in the trash can, the fun stops. Those at the bottom get stuck with the bill.

Despot or Friend?

The knee-jerk response to revenue problems caused by falling fertility, such as Social Security has experienced, has been to raise taxes. This, however, further undermines the support base of Social Security because higher taxes make it more difficult financially for couples to have children.

It is still possible, though increasingly difficult, to sustain a family in this country on a single wage. Parents are not so lucky in Sweden. The welfare state there consumes such large chunks of personal income that both husband and wife almost are forced to work. The Swedes may have brought this statist nightmare upon themselves, but they apparently are less than enchanted with the results. A 1984 survey of Swedes showed eighty-one percent were in agreement that "the state has become increasingly despotic at the expense of individual rights."[10]

The trend of tax rates in the United States has been arguably despotic, at least from a Christian perspective. When the state demands a total tax that exceeds ten percent, as modern taxes do by a long shot, it is considered by some to be idolatrous because it is asking more than the tithe (ten percent) that God asks of His people. This is bad enough.

What is less obvious is how our income tax structure is antagonistic toward the Biblical favor on procreation. Bryce Christensen, writing in the Rockford Institute's *Family in America* newsletter, notes that the evolution of the federal income tax in recent decades has discouraged couples from having children.

> The average Federal income tax rate of a traditional family with four children increased by *223 percent* between 1960 and 1984, while during the same years the tax load borne by singles did not increase at all.[11] If the personal income tax exemption had kept pace with inflation, it would today stand at about $5,100 (italics in original).[12]

A 1992 Rockford Institute publication put that last figure at $8,260.[13] Instead, the personal exemption for many years stood at $1,000 and increased only slightly to $1,040 in 1985 and $1,800 in 1986. Then the Tax Reform Act of 1986 changed that to $1,900 in 1987 and $2,150 by 1992. Much better, but still only a fourth of the $8,260 it should be to have maintained the earlier ratio.

If you have ever computed your personal income tax, you know how that kind of spread of personal exemptions translates. It means that thanks to those under-scaled exemptions, you probably are paying several hundred, if not a couple thousand dollars a year more in taxes, depending on your tax bracket and the number of dependents. The state needs new generations to maintain a healthy economy, a strong military, and a sound Social Security system, yet the tax rate has increasingly made children a financial burden for couples.

As Christensen points out, singles did not experience this increasing tax burden over the last four decades. And not only singles, but childless couples and single-parent families have all tended to gain tax benefits while greater loads are shifted to a dwindling proportion of traditional families (two spouses, one income, with children). In effect, our tax code has evolved to where it penalizes successful, intact families and rewards every form of non-traditional family.

For example, child-care allowances have been granted to mothers who work outside the home but denied to mothers who labor just as hard at home with children.

> In effect, this forces traditional parents to pay higher taxes for the privilege of caring for their own children. Because a number of studies have concluded that day care turns children into more aggressive, less cooperative adults than does traditional parenting,[14] this tax penalty imposed for stay-at-home mothering seems not only unjust but foolish.[15]

Imagine the harried mother of preschoolers who is determined to stay home with her kids, to give them the quantity of time and early education that has proven to be invaluable. She could use a break. Yet if she arranges for a weekly day of paid care to preserve her energy and enable her to press on, there is no tax break. If she chooses to go to work, she gets to double-dip: a paycheck from her employer and a tax break from Uncle Sam. When our laws discourage women from specializing in motherhood, the status of children is clear. They are considered burdens, not blessings.

The legal system has further devalued children by making divorce easier. One study shows that the standard of living of divorced women and their children drops by seventy-three percent a year after the divorce.[16] This is another rotten fruit from the tree of feminism. They demanded the freedom for easy and quick divorce, and they got it—along with poverty.

They also gave the same easy exit to unprincipled men, who found their standard of living increased forty-two percent,[17] and who could not resist the temptation to jettison a used wife in favor of a newer (younger) model. And for the majority of women who lack the marketable skills of feminist lawyers, lobbyists, and journalists, especially when they are over thirty-five or forty, the new "freedom" of divorce has been no glory ride. Unwanted by employers and men, they face a long, dismal future.

It's bad enough for such women. It's worse for their children. Not only do the kids have to share in their mother's poverty, but studies have shown

> that children of divorced parents are much more likely to suffer from emotional and mental problems and are much less likely to perform well in school than are children from intact homes.[18] Such troubled children necessarily demand more attention from teachers, police, judges and mental health officials, all paid out of public funds.[19]

Again, these public funds are disproportionately confiscated from the earnings of married couples with children. As the welfare program has mushroomed since the 1960s, it is those who reject traditional family who have received the most benefits: divorced women, single parents and their children (including illegitimate ones), and the unemployed. It is traditional families, with higher earnings and more stable workers, who are feeding the welfare machine but getting very little of its produce.

Isolating the Generations

We've seen that the mere existence of a state-run pension program is a disincentive for having children. This was confirmed in a study of eighty-one countries. It showed that, where a social security system is broad and well-funded, fertility is low. When the government pension system is weak, fertility is high.[20] If the government's going to take care of you when you get old, why bother raising children?

America's Social Security tax is certainly among those that discourage fertility.

First, there is no personal exemption applied to the tax. You and your spouse can sweat and spend like crazy to raise your children—future supporters of the Social Security fund—but it makes no difference on how much you are taxed for the program. Your childless neighbor couple, taking annual ski trips to Colorado on that extra disposable income, pays the same rate. When you and your neighbors are drawing Social Security benefits, they will be skimming the cream from a trust fund sustained by a work force produced by you and other parents.

Second, Social Security taxes are no longer a negligible pinch out of family income. In 1992, the rate was 15.3 percent (for the self-employed, or 7.65 percent on the employer and 7.65 percent on the employee). Furthermore, the tax is extracted from the first dollars earned (up to $55,500 in 1992). Even those with incomes low enough to avoid income taxes have to chip in for Social Security. While there can be argued a certain fairness to that, it also means a greater financial burden, proportionally, on young couples whose income is low. It is more difficult for them to raise children or to save in order to buy a house to accommodate a family. For many such couples, the answer is to wait much longer to have children or to remain childless. Meanwhile, the retirement program is jeopardized that much further as its support base shrivels.

One of the sad things about Social Security is that Americans have come to rely upon it so much, yet it falls so short of meeting retirement needs. To supplement Social Security, financial planners recommend a sizable savings program; other sources recognize the age-old wisdom of having children to provide old-age care.

Money magazine, quoting an *American Demographics* editor, agreed that "the best long-term investment for a baby-boom couple will be to have children." The reasons: prolonged retirement and a crippled Social Security structure mean bleak retirement years for all but the wealthy—or well-propagated. Families, the article noted, typically provide eighty percent of the nursing care and personal services for those over eighty-five with disabilities.[21]

Germaine Greer cites the writing of Elizabeth Warnock Fernea, the wife of an American anthropologist working in Iraq. The Iraqi women, who revered their elderly, asked her if it was true "that in America they put all the old women in houses by themselves, away from their families." Ms. Fernea's reply that, yes, that is sometimes true, drew disapproval from the Iraqi women. They were used to a culture that rewarded elderly women with "response and respect as members of their children's households."[22]

Now, with Social Security entrenched both as an entitlement and as an excuse for middle-aged children to neglect their parents, it is too common for senior citizens to live alone, to die alone. This happens even when family members are living in the same community. Jesus condemned those who dedicated their financial gifts as "Corban," or earmarked for the temple, while their parents suffered in poverty (Mark 7:9-13). Not just money, but time, love, service in your home—these assets must not be withheld from aging relatives in need. It is not always feasible, for medical or emotional reasons, to bring parents into a home. But to abandon the aged, when against their will and not absolutely necessary, is detestable when children are capable of fulfilling their final phase as blessings by caring for those who cared so well for them in earlier days.

Against the Tide

The reckless death spirit of Pharaoh, Herod, and Hitler is alive and well, though less recognized. While history records many examples of pro-natalist government policies, the modern thrust is typified by the communists of China, the liberal socialism of Sweden, and the quasi-socialism of the United States.

America is not that far behind those other two nations. When our government legalizes abortion and winks at occasional infanticide, when it drafts a tax structure that discourages procreation, when it continues to expand a parasitic welfare system that uses healthy families as its host, it has declared itself the enemy of the traditional family that sees children as a blessing.

Christians, therefore, must fight to change codified anti-natalism. Prayer comes first. Then there are other avenues to pursue. We must support political candidates who will unequivocally defend the sanctity of life in and out of the womb and the rights of parents everywhere to regulate their own fertility without state interference. We must support candidates who will endorse pro-family tax measures and who are clear-sighted enough to fight for *truly* pro-family positions regarding the myriad proposals related to family and abortion that will be debated in Congress and state legislatures during the 1990s. On these same issues, we should let ourselves be known with letters to elected officials and letters to newspaper and magazine editors. We should support local pro-life counseling centers and halfway homes for young single mothers; when possible, we should open our homes to those mothers. It is our obligation to preserve a legal and social climate where God's people are free to fulfill the Biblical mandate to multiply and subdue the earth without interference.

More important, Christians must prove themselves doers of the Word, not mere hearers. We must look to the long term in raising children to permeate the "child-free" society as blessers in every respect. The two short psalms we will examine next confirm the wonderful blessing that God intends for families and communities through the gift of new births.

PART 6

THE CONCLUSION

Twelve

Prosperity and Posterity

Indeed, may you see your children's children. Peace be upon Israel!

Psalm 128:6

Are you prosperous? How do you know for sure?

The paycheck is certainly an important indicator. Then there are assets—money in the bank, real estate, stocks, and cars. And you can weigh those against debts of credit cards, car notes, and house payments.

The Bible has strong things to say about wealth and debt. Yet there is no magic level of income, no set ratio of assets to debt, by which one can declare prosperity has arrived.

There are, however, passages that describe prosperity from God's perspective, such as Psalms 127 and 128. These back-to-back psalms say nothing about money, jewels, BMWs, beach condos, or anything else most of us would tend to put on our laundry list of the Quintessentials of Prosperity. Rather these verses extol the blessing of children and the fruitful family. God says prosperity is bound up in these.

As we examine Psalms 127 and 128, we will see how marvelously they confirm the often surprising truths we have uncovered regarding procreation, blessing and population growth. They deal with five areas of blessing:

• God as the source of blessing.
• Children as a blessing and reward from God.
• The transmission of godly blessings through children.
• Children as direct blessings to their parents.
• God's blessing on the community through fruitful families.

All in Vain

"Vanity of vanities! All is vanity," ranted the Preacher in the opening (1:2) of Ecclesiastes. (Perhaps he had been cleaning the kitchen floor after his kids had finished their nightly redistribution of food that decent families call supper.) Psalm 127:1-2 warns further of vain activity:

Unless the Lord builds the house,
They labor in vain who build it;
Unless the Lord guards the city,
The watchman keeps awake in vain.
It is vain for you to rise up early,
To retire late,
To eat the bread of painful labors;
For He gives to His beloved even in his sleep.

No, this does not mean you can quit your job and your merciful heavenly Father will supply all your needs according to His riches in glory in Christ Jesus, Amen. Nor does it mean you can quit the vain, endless tasks such as cleaning that kitchen floor. In other places, Scripture endorses work and the just connection between reaping and sowing.

The authors of Ecclesiastes and Psalm 127 are emphasizing the uselessness of striving for blessing apart from God. We twentieth-century New Testament folks would call it trying to achieve something in the flesh.

When man thinks he can orchestrate blessing merely by limiting family size, he is mistaken. As the example of China shows, not only does a state-enforced plan fail to produce blessings, it is beginning to reap uncounted horrors—abortion and infanticide of epic proportions, and a social imbalance between generations that will disrupt society for at least a few decades. China's demographic "watchmen," along with the nosy village monitors and the ruthless clinic butchers, stay awake in vain to conjure blessings. God is not building their house.

God, instead, chooses to rain blessing upon "His beloved even in his sleep," when he is expecting no payoff. While the "beloved" of God may not have *earned* blessing per se, he can justly hope for as much because God is faithful to keep promises.

So this is the first theme: *God is the source of all blessings.*

It constitutes a simple thread running through both Old and New Testaments. That is, obey your part of the covenant, and God will honor His. Fear God and walk in His way, as Psalm 128:1-2 explains:

> How blessed is everyone who fears the Lord,
> Who walks in His ways.
> When you shall eat of the fruit of your hands,
> You will be happy and it will be well with you.

This also speaks to the overpopulation worries. Those arguments focus on pessimism more than optimism, on consumption more than production, on degradation more than innovation.

What happens when an economy is unfettered by exorbitant tax rates, government-subsidized competition, and burdensome regulations? In most cases, there is creativity, growth, and prosperity. All except the sluggards work, eat the fruit of their hands, and it is well with them. Housing, food production, transportation, and every other segment adjusts to the growing population. There will be poverty and other problems, but population growth is not the cause of those problems. Population growth, fueling demand and new opportunities, is a blessing.

To summarize, it is vanity for the state or any anti-natalist organization to try to fabricate blessings for mankind by suppressing fertility. Sovereign God alone can bless.

Arrows, Grapes, and Olive Plants

When the Bible talks about God's blessings, it often speaks of fruitfulness. It is no accident that Deuteronomy 6 refers to fruitful herds, fruitful crops, and fruitful women in the same breath. Likewise, images of fertility—vine and olive plants (or shoots)—are used in a favorable light in Psalm 128. Continuing to describe the household of the righteous, prosperous man, who is happy and enjoying the fruits of his labor, Psalm 128:3-4 says:

> Your wife shall be like a fruitful vine,
> Within your house,
> Your children like olive plants
> Around your table.
> Behold, for thus shall the man be blessed
> Who fears the Lord.

Procreation is no option in the Bible's description of a blessed household. Whatever other occupation the wife may have had—and in the day this was written there was less segmentation between household work and commercial work because commerce tended to be home-centered—she was also occupied with child raising.

That she would conceive was by no means taken for granted. Hence, the second theme: *Children are altogether gift, reward, and blessing from God to their parents.* Psalm 127:3-5a says:

> Behold, children are a gift of the Lord;
> The fruit of the womb is a reward.
> Like arrows in the hand of a warrior,
> So are the children of one's youth.
> How blessed is the man whose quiver is full
>   of them.

Is everyone's quiver the same size? How do you know when yours is full? Scripture offers no set answer, but obviously childlessness or one child is less than the plural arrows or children mentioned in the psalm. The context stresses fullness. In a *general* sense, we can assume the more children, the bigger the blessing. As Jesus said, our heavenly Father, like an earthly father, gives only good gifts to His children.

Inheritances and Crowns

Everyone likes getting a gift. Trouble is, most gifts don't last, or at least not very long. Money gifts, even big amounts, get spent. Food gifts get eaten. Clothes wear out. Appliances break.

Saying children are a "gift" from the Lord (Ps. 127:3) is too limiting. This gift is more than a one-time affair. Other translations of Ps. 127:3 more properly render the word as *heritage* of the Lord. The Hebrew word includes the ideas of heirloom, inheritance, and estate. Rather than a gift to be consumed and forgotten, children are personalized assets that involve the parents in at least three generations. They represent God's blessing because they ensure that the parents' own heritage, or lineage, will continue. The precious possession of the family name will not die out.

Without children, it would be impossible for adults to give the blessing—both in a material and spiritual sense—described in Proverbs 13:22: "A good man leaves an inheritance to his children's children." And without children, it would be impossible to receive the blessing spoken of in Proverbs 17:6: "Grandchildren are the crown of old men." Children are intended to be the gift that keeps on giving. Here is the third theme of these two psalms: *Children are a blessing because they facilitate the transfer of godly heritage between generations.*

Guardians at the Gate

Psalm 127's comparison of children to arrows in a quiver is not happenstance. Arrows were the weapon of the day in ancient Israel. They killed enemies. They protected against attackers. Occasionally they may have felled game and provided food. Psalm 127:4-5 declares:

> Like arrows in the hand of a warrior,
> So are the children of one's youth.
> How blessed is the man whose quiver is full
>   of them;
> They shall not be ashamed,
> When they speak with their enemies in the
>   gate.

Is this to say we should reckon children as budding soldiers? Yes, but not merely in the military sense—though that is nothing to shrug off. Throughout history, nations have worried about maintaining their power when their populations have declined. Even today, nuclear weapons may threaten and deter, but it is warm bodies who perform the bread and butter of maintaining bases, fleets, and reserve units.

More to the point, children are also arrows in the sense that they should be defenders of their family, especially of their parents. Psalm 127:4 refers to the children of one's youth, meaning that a crop of kids born early will be mature and productive that much sooner. If the parents were to fall into bad health, if the wife were to lose her husband, grown-up children were then—and still can be today—the best insurance available. Adult children would provide housing, food, fellowship, and basic care. They would be the ones to defend parents inside the city gate (127:5), where enemies or those who brought charges would go for judicial resolution. So the fourth theme: *Children bless their parents by adding to their strength.*

Boaz, in the Bible, went to the city gate to act on behalf of an elderly woman, Naomi. She had had a run of hard times. First, she lost her husband. Then her two sons died. One daughter-in-law returned to her mother's house; the other, Ruth, stuck with her. Naomi, an aging widow without sons, was prepared to sell land that had belonged to her deceased husband, Elimelech, when Boaz came on the scene.

Boaz became interested in Ruth, but he also was aware of another relative who had the first rights of redemption for Naomi's land. The relative at first agreed to buy the land. Then, when informed that the package also included Ruth and the levirate marriage obligation to raise children through her for her late husband, Mahlon, he passed. The investment of raising a family with Ruth, along with buying the land only to hold it in trust for the son she would probably bear, would have caused him, he said, to "jeopardize my own inheritance" (Ruth 4:6).

So Boaz seized the whole deal. The land was sold. Ruth got a new husband. Naomi got plugged into a household with a prosperous male head. The witnesses at the gate prayed that Ruth would be "like Rachel and Leah" (4:11) and that the house of Ruth and Boaz would be fruitful (4:12). Boaz, a son-in-law-to-be, became a blessing to Naomi.

Incidentally, when a child came, it was not the mother who received the attention, it was the grandmother:

> Then the women said to Naomi, "Blessed is the Lord who has not left you without a redeemer today, and may his name become famous in Israel. May he also be to you a restorer of life and a sustainer of your old age; for your daughter-in-law, who loves you and is better to you than seven sons, has given birth to him" (4:14-15).

> And the neighbor women gave him a name, saying, "A son has been born to Naomi!" (4:17).

Boaz was not ashamed to speak on behalf of his relative in the city gate. He was not reluctant to act, even though it may have meant financial loss over the years as he held the land in trust and took on two dependent women. The result was enhanced status and prosperity for Ruth and her mother-in-law. Ultimately there was blessing for all of Israel, even all of Christendom: Ruth's son Obed became grandfather of King David.

The neighbor women's prayer for Naomi's grandchild says a lot: May he restore, or renew, your life and sustain you in your old age. Many elderly people in America, unfortunately, can testify that life is dull and meaningless because they have no children, or those they have ignore them. A study that has traced people who are now in their eighties shows that not only the marital bond but the parent-child bond has been able "to provide greater and greater levels of satisfaction as the participants age."[1] They are sustained, emotionally, in their old age.

We no longer have literal city gates where disputes are resolved. But we do have city councils, state legislatures, a national Congress, and a sprawling system of courts. We have school boards, zoning boards, and corporate boards of directors. There is no question but that someone will fill every seat on those bodies. There will be votes cast, laws proposed, justice meted. The mature arrows from a former generation will be piercing the future, forming the cultural and legal climate for years to come. Every generation has the choice to bring arrows into their quivers, to aim them with precision by way of careful training, and to loose them on the world. If Christian couples passively dodge their responsibility to fill their quivers and prayerfully focus the path of their arrows, they help to abdicate their society to God's enemies.

We have Jesus as our model. Isaiah, speaking prophetically of the Messiah, said: "And He has also made Me a select arrow; He has hidden Me in His quiver" (Is. 49:2b) and "He has made My mouth like a sharp sword" (49:2a). Jesus was not afraid to unsheathe His verbal sword to duel with God's enemies in the gate. He stood up to the Romans, the civil powers of the day. He was fond of needling the scribes and Pharisees, calling them hypocrites to their faces. After God the Father let loose His bowstring that brought the messianic arrow into the world, the kingdom of darkness suffered a blow from which it never recovered. Each Christian child holds similar potential in the spirit: to follow in Christ's footsteps, piercing the kingdom of darkness, advancing the kingdom of light.

It may not be every child that does so. The Bible has many general promises that righteous training will produce righteous young adults. But God gives no money-back guarantee that one hundred percent of the children born to Christian couples will turn out to be sweet, spiritual, or even saved. It may be the last child, the marginal "surprise," or the conception that was allowed when common sense hollered otherwise, who carries God's special favor. It was David, the eighth and youngest son of Jesse, who was anointed king of Israel.

Also, it may not even be the first generation of your children that fulfills all you hope for. A prophecy came to the great-grandfather of James Dobson that four generations of his family would serve the Lord. Sure enough, each generation was involved with ministry. When James Dobson's father was sixty-six, in ill health and not as active in his ministry as before, the senior Dobson prayed for three days and nights that God would extend the ministries and lives of him and his dying brother. Dobson recalls how God responded to his father's requests:

> He told him, "I have heard your prayers; I know that you are concerned about My people and My kingdom. I know your compassion, and I'm going to answer your prayers. In fact, you're going to reach millions of people. But

it is not going to be through you. It will be through your son."[2]

The next day, James Dobson Sr. had a massive heart attack. He died seventy-two days later.

"Millions of people" proved to be no exaggeration. Dobson's eight-part "Focus on the Family" film series has been seen by an estimated fifty million people. His talk show is aired on more than 1,100 radio stations daily. The Focus on the Family headquarters receives about six thousand letters a day. When Dobson speaks at the city gate, it may be that of Washington, D.C., where the Focus-supported Family Research Council has become one of the most influential lobbyists for traditional family values.

Four generations of Dobsons were taken from the quiver and shot in service of the Lord. Yet it was the great-grandchild that packed a nuclear warhead on the arrow.

Shalom, Everybody

Ministries of Dobson's magnitude are critical for impacting society and advancing Christ's kingdom. At the same time, they would be in vain without the faithful labor of families willing to till their own humble fields. The closing of Psalm 128 contains the kind of verses we tend to skim in Bible reading, but there is rich content. The verses summarize Psalms 127 and 128:

> The Lord bless you from Zion,
> And may you see the prosperity of Jerusalem
> all the days of your life.

> Indeed, may you see your children's children.
> Peace be upon Israel! (128:5-6)

Blessings are not man-made, but flow from the king of Mount Zion. Not just individual families, but the community (like Jerusalem) and the nation (like Israel) can be expected to prosper when families are fruitful and walking in righteousness before that king. The blessing of seeing Jerusalem's prosperity and the blessing of seeing one's grandchildren go hand in hand. It is taken for granted that in a prosperous civilization, families are expanding, helping build a strong, secure community. Such a culture makes it more possible for citizens to survive into old age, where they will enjoy the fellowship and support of their children and grandchildren.

The "peace" wished upon Israel is the familiar Hebrew *shalom*. As "peace" it means not just an absence of war, but the fullness of prosperity, health, and happiness. This general sense of *shalom* fits the climate of a prosperous, steadily growing society: security in government, creation of jobs, expansion of capital, innovations in science and culture, and continuing demand in all markets.

This is the final theme of these psalms: *God uses fruitful families to bless society.*

Large families and growing populations do not automatically evidence God's favor. India, for example, has one of the world's largest populations, and it is still growing. Yet it has not emerged as a world-class economic or military contender.

But when God's people look to Him for blessings (Ps. 127:1-2), when they fear Him and walk in His ways (Ps. 128:1), they should expect the blessing of fruitful families. Furthermore, they should not try to reject what God calls blessing by unreasonably limiting fertility. Such striving to hoard material blessings and to refuse to share them with many (or any) children is based on man's vain valuations. In the end, it is destined to disappoint.

Instead, we have another choice: to reckon children as a gift, a heritage, a reward, an ever-appreciating asset. It does not come naturally for some. It does not come without work for anybody. And it takes time for the investment to pay off in full. But the blessing does come for those willing to pioneer as parents, those willing to train up their children in righteousness, those willing to try to pray them through where all else fails.

And I promise this: No matter how rough it gets, you won't get lonely or bored. And you'll have fond memories, yea, even wild tales to spin to your children's children. Shalom!

ENDNOTES

Chapter 1:
The Flight From Procreation

1. Robert Coughlan, *The Wine of Genius* (New York: Harper & Brothers, Publishers) pp. 45-46, in Germaine Greer, *Sex and Destiny* (London, England: Martin Secker & Warburg Limited, 1984), p. 7.
2. Martha Smilgis, "The Dilemmas of Childlessness," *Time*, May 2, 1988, p. 88.
3. Lois Duncan, "Families in the '80s: Is Bigger Better?," *Woman's Day*, November 22, 1988, p. 62.
4. Ben Wattenberg, *The Birth Dearth* (New York: Pharos Books, 1987), p. 16.
5. "Urban Population Explosion," *Christianity Today*, May 16, 1986, p. 52.
6. Allan C. Carlson, "Religion and Family: The Troubled and Enduring Bond," *The Family in America*, January 1988, p. 6.
7. Gordon F. De Jong, "Religious Fundamentalism, Socio-Economic Status, and Fertility Attitudes in the Southern Appalachians," *Demography* 2 (1965): pp. 540-549; Michael Lee Yoder, "Religion as a Determinant of Fertility Among White Americans, 1965," doctoral dissertation (University of Wisconsin-Madison, 1980), pp. 230, 235; cited in Carlson, "Religion and Family: The Troubled and Enduring Bond," p. 7.

8. William H. Willimon, "Children: The Blessed Burden," *Religion in Life*, Spring 1980, p. 24.
9. Information listed here is found in Wattenberg, p. 119-129.

Chapter 2:
Abandoned Preschoolers, Dormant Teens

1. Carol Polsgrove, "One Mother's Search for Child Care," *The Progressive*, November 1988, p. 16.
2. *Ibid.*, p. 18.
3. George Gilder, "An Open Letter to Orrin Hatch," *National Review*, May 13, 1988, p. 34.
4. U.S. Bureau of the Census, *Statistical Abstract of the United States: 1987*, 107th ed. (Washington: U.S. Bureau of the Census, 1986), pp. 367, 383, cited in Bryce J. Christensen, "Day Care: Thalidomide of the 1980's?" *The Family in America*, November 1987, pp. 1-7.
5. Christensen, "Day Care: Thalidomide of the 1980's?," p. 1-7.
6. Connaught Marshner, "Socialized Motherhood: As Easy as ABC," *National Review*, May 13, 1988, p. 30.
7. David E. Bloom and Todd P. Steen, "Why Child Care Is Good for Business," *American Demographics*, August 1988, p. 25.
8. 1985 study by psychologist Ron Haskins of the University of North Carolina, in Christensen, "Day Care: Thalidomide of the 1980's?," p. 5.

9. Study by researchers from Pritzker School of Medicine and the University of Illinois, cited in Christensen, "Day Care: Thalidomide of the 1980's?," p. 5.

10. Research of psychologist Jay Belsky, cited in Christensen, "Day Care: Thalidomide of the 1980's?," p. 5.

11. *Ibid.*

12. Pitirim Sorokin, *Social and Cultural Dynamics: A Study of Change in Major Systems of Art, Truth, Ethics, Law, and Social Relationships* (1957; rpt. New Brunswick: Transaction, 1985), pp. 700-701, cited in Christensen, "Day Care: Thalidomide of the 1980's?," p. 7.

13. Deborah L. Vandell and Mary A. Corasaniti, "Variations in Early Child Care: Do They Predict Subsequent Social, Emotional, and Cognitive Differences?," then current in press, cited in "Dangers of Day Care," *The Family in America New Research*, October 1988, p. 3.

14. Georges Peter, *et. al.*, eds., *Report of the Committee on Infectious Diseases* (Elk Grove, Ill.: American Academy of Pediatrics, 1986), pp. 54-58; Stanley H. Schuman, "Day Care Associated Infection: More Than Meets the Eye," (f2)Journal of the American Medical Association(f1), 249, No. 1 (January 7, 1983), p. 76; Stephen R. Redmond and Michael E. Pichichero, "Hemophilus Influenza Type B Disease: An Epidemiologic Study With Special References to Day Care Centers," *Journal of the American Medical Association*, 252 (November 9, 1984), pp. 2581-2584; Robert E. Black, "Giardiasis in

Day Care Centers: Evidence of Person-to-Person Transmission," *Pediatrics*, 60, No. 4 (October 1977), pp. 486-489; Stephen C. Hadler, *et. al.*, "Hepatitis A in Day Care Centers," *New England Journal of Medicine*, 302, No. 72 (May 29, 1980), pp. 1222-1227; cited in Christensen, "Day Care: Thalidomide of the 1980's?," p. 4.

15. *Ibid.*
16. *Ibid.*
17. *Ibid.*
18. Edward M. Levine, "Day Care: Cons, Costs, Kids," *Chicago Tribune* September 18, 1984, Sec. 1, p. 15, cited in Christensen, "Day Care: Thalidomide of the 1980's?," p. 6.
19. Harold M. Voth, MD., "The Role of the Family in Nurturing the Child for Responsible Adulthood," in *The Family: America's Hope* (Rockford, Ill.: Rockford College Institute, 1979), p. 68.
20. C. John Sommerville, *The Rise and Fall of Childhood* (Beverly Hills, Calif.: Sage Publications Inc., 1982), p. 179.
21. Edwin Kiester Jr. and Sally Valente Kiester, "How to Raise a Happy Child," *Reader's Digest* reprint from January 1986.
22. *Ibid.*
23. "Kids crave money, fame," *The Tuscaloosa News*, September 28, 1986, p. 18A. (Some information used in Chapter 2 was deleted from this New York Times News Service story as it appeared in *The Tuscaloosa News*.)
24. Susan Littwin, *The Postponed Generation* (New York: William Morrow and Company, Inc., 1986), p. 100.

Chapter 3:
Be Fruitful and Multiply

1. Gary North, *The Dominion Covenant: Genesis* (Tyler, Texas: The Institute for Christian Economics, 1982), p. 100.
2. *Ibid.*, p. 164.

Chapter 4:
The Hebrew Family

1. Encyclopedia Judaica, s.v. "family," p. 1172.
2. Johannes Pedersen, *Israel: Its Life and Culture* (Vol. I), London: Geoffrey Cumberledge Oxford University Press, 1926, p. 209.
3. "Three's a Crowd," *Newsweek*, September 1, 1986, p. 71.
4. Pedersen, *Israel: Its Life and Culture* (Vol. I), p. 206.
5. *Ibid.*, p. 207.
6. *Ibid.*
7. *Encyclopedia Judaica*, p. 1171.
8. North, *The Dominion Covenant: Genesis*, p. 162.
9. Norman Lobsenz, "Should a Wife Keep Her Name?" *Parade*, December 7, 1986, p. 8.
10. Pedersen, *Israel: Its Life and Culture* (Vol. I), p. 254.
11. *Ibid.*, p. 255.
12. *Ibid.*, p. 79.
13. Mayer Eisenstein, M.D., "Religion in Support of the Family: A Jewish Commentary," in *The Family: America's Hope* (Rockford, Ill.: Rockford College Institute, 1979), p. 68.

14. *Ibid.*
15. *Ibid.*, p. 69.
16. *Ibid.*, p. 70.

Chapter 5:
Birth Control:
Right or Wrong?

1. John T. Noonan Jr., *Contraception: A History of Its Treatment by the Catholic Theologians and Canonists* (Cambridge, Mass. and London, England: The Belknap Press of Harvard University Press, 1965, enlarged edition), p. 9.
2. David M. Feldman, *Marital Relations, Birth Control, and Abortion in Jewish Law* (New York: Schocken Books, 1968), p. 152.
3. Noonan, *Contraception*, p. 36.
4. Feldman, *Marital Relations, Birth Control, and Abortion in Jewish Law*, p. 145.
5. Noonan, *Contraception*, p. 58.
6. *The Westminster Dictionary of Christian Ethics*, s.v. "procreation."
7. *New Catholic Encyclopedia*, s.v. "birth control movement."
8. Greer, *Sex and Destiny*, p. 297.
9. Allan C. Carlson, "The Sensual School," *Persuasion at Work*, July 1986, pp. 2-5.
10. *Ibid.*, pp. 2-3.
11. *Ibid.*, p. 3.
12. *Ibid.*

13. Jack Douglas, "The Sexual Modernists," *The Family in America*, May 1987, p. 3.
14. Greer, *Sex and Destiny,* p. 303.
15. *Ibid.*
16. Carlson, "The Sensual School," p. 3.
17. Margaret Sanger in Carlson, "The Sensual School," p. 3.
18. Carlson, "The Sensual School," p. 3.
19. Greer, *Sex and Destiny*, p. 304.
20. Carlson, "The Sensual School," p. 3.
21. *Ibid.*
22. Greer, *Sex and Destiny*, p. 303.
23. *Ibid.*, p. 309.
24. *Ibid.*, p. 310.
25. Carlson, "The Sensual School," p. 4.
26. *Ibid.*, p. 4
27. *Ibid.*, pp. 4-5.
28. *Ibid.*, p. 5.
29. Richard N. Ostling, "John Paul's Feisty Flock," *Time*, September 7, 1987, p. 48.
30. Bill Gothard, *Advanced Seminar Textbook* (Institute of Basic Youth Conflicts, 1986), pp. 172-197.
31. Mary Pride, *The Way Home: Beyond Feminism and Back to Reality* (Westchester, Ill.: Crossway Books, a division of Good News Publishers, 1985), p. 29.
32. Arnold G. Fruchtenbaum, *Hebrew Christianity: Its Theology, History and Philosophy* (Grand Rapids, Mich.: Baker Book House, 1974), p. 89.

Chapter 6:
Birth Control:
Building a Better Incubator

1. Gothard, *Advanced Seminar Textbook*, p. 201.
2. *Ibid.*, p. 202.
3. Duncan, "Families in the '80s: Is Bigger Better?," p. 201.
4. "How Big Families Make It Work," *Woman's Day*, November 22, 1988, p. 61.

Chapter 7:
Motherhood:
The Neglected Career

1. Bloom and Steen, "Why Child Care Is Good for Business," p. 22.
2. Horst H. Stipp, "What Is a Working Woman?", *American Demographics*, July 1988, p. 27.
3. Herbert J. Gans, *The Levittowners* (New York: Pantheon, 1967), and Helen Z. Lopata, *Occupation Housewife* (New York: Oxford University Press, 1971), p. 376, cited in George Gilder, *Men and Marriage* (Gretna, La.: Pelican Publishing Co., 1986), p. 167.
4. *Life*, special issue on the Constitution, Fall 1987, p. 32.
5. Midge Yearly, "The Early American Women," *The Atlanta Journal and Constitution*, October 17, 1976, cited in Carl W. Wilson, *Our Dance Has Turned to Death: But We Can Renew the*

Family and Nation (Tyndale House Publishers, Living Books, 1981), p. 57.

6. *Ibid.*

7. Allan C. Carlson, "Work and Family: On a Collision Course in America?" *Persuasion at Work*, May 1986, pp. 2-3.

8. *Ibid.*, p. 3.

9. *Ibid.*

10. "Time Off for the Family," *The Family in America: New Research,* November 1987, p. 1.

11. Carol Iannone, "Analyzing a Feminist Whine," (f2)The American Spectator(f1), May 1988, p. 30.

12. Shulamith Firestone, *The Dialectic of Sex: The Case for Feminist Revolution* (New York: William Morrow, 1970), pp. 233-40, 272, cited in "The Androgyny Hoax," by Allan C. Carlson, *Persuasion at Work*, March 1986, p. 3.

13. *Ibid.*

14. Voth, "The Role of the Family in Nurturing the Child for Responsible Adulthood," p. 31.

15. Pride, *The Way Home*, pp. 41-42.

16. *Ibid.*, p. 42.

17. *Ibid.*, pp. 142-152.

Chapter 8:
Parenthood's Deep
Currents of Blessings

1. Joe Levin, "Fighting the Silent Attacker," *Time*, December 1, 1986, p. 64.

2. R.V. Short, "The evolution of home reproduction," *Proceedings of the Royal Society of London*, B, Vol 195 (1976), p. 20, cited in Greer, *Sex and Destiny*, p. 157.
3. Gilder, *Men and Marriage*, p. 5.
4. *Ibid.*, pp. 176-177.
5. Julian Simon, *The Ultimate Resource*, (Princeton, N.J.: Princeton University Press, 1981), p. 260.
6. Stephen Koepp, "Fighting the Urge to Splurge," *Time*, December 14, 1987, p. 58.
7. James Hitchcock, "The Family as a Stabilizing Force in the Life of an Adult," *The Family: America's Hope*, p. 50.

Chapter 9:
Growing Populations:
Their Benefits, Their Enemies

1. R.E. McMaster Jr., "No Time for Slaves" (Phoenix, Ariz.: Reaper Publishing, 1986), pp. 148-149.
2. *Ibid.*
3. Paul Ehrlich, in Tom Bethell, "Imperialism and the Pill," *National Review*, March 14, 1986, p. 38.
4. Bethell, "Imperialism and the Pill," p. 38.
5. Donella H. Meadows, Dennis L. Meadows, Jorgen Randers, William W. Behrens III, *The Limits to Growth* (New York: The New American Library, 1974), back cover.
6. *Ibid.*, inside page.
7. Simon, *The Ultimate Resource*, p. 286.

8. *Ibid.*, p. 287.
9. Information listed here is found in Simon, pp. 174-348.
10. Max Heine, "Food is great, but freedom's much better," *The Tuscaloosa News*, June 30, 1985, p. 25A.
11. *World Book*, 1985, s.v. "China," "India," "Japan," "Taiwan," "United States."
12. Simon, *The Ultimate Resource*, p. 292.
13. Greer, *Sex and Destiny*, p. 414-415.
14. Based on Population Reference Bureau, *World Population Growth and Response: 1965-1975—A Decade of Global Action* (Washington: The Population Reference Bureau, April 1976), pp. 226-227; and Agency for International Development, *Rationale for AID Support of Population Programs*, January 1982, p. 24; and World Bank, *World Development Report 1984*, pp. 148, 180-181; cited in Jacqueline Kasun, *The War Against Population: The Economics and Ideology of World Population Control* (San Francisco: Ignatius Press, 1988), p. 79.
15. U.S. Government document, NSSM 200, "Implications of Worldwide Population Growth for U.S. Security and Overseas Interests," December 10, 1974, declassified December 31, 1980, p. 14; cited in Kasun, *The War Against Population*, pp. 79-80.
16. Kasun, *The War Against Population*, pp. 79-94.
17. *St. Louis Post-Dispatch*, April 22, 1977, p. 1, cited in Kasun, *The War Against Population*, p. 81.

18. Robert S. McNamara in *Christian Science Monitor* interview, July 5, 1977; cited in Kasun, *The War Against Population*, p. 81.
19. AID 1976 policy paper on "U.S. Population Related Assistance," and Select Committee on Population, *Report*, "Population and Development Assistance," U.S. House of Representatives, 95th Congress, 2nd Session (Washington: U.S. Government Printing Office, 1978), p. 100, cited in Kasun, *The War Against Population*, p. 83.
20. The World Bank, *World Development Report 1980* (Washington, 1980), p. 80; The Population Council, *Studies in Family Planning*, Vol. 5, No. 5, May 1974, pp. 148-151, and Vol. 7, No. 7, July 1976, pp. 188-196, and September 1978; Select Committee on Population, *Report*, op. cit., p. 70; cited in Kasun, *The War Against Population*, p. 84.
21. The Population Council, (f2)Studies in Family Planning(f1), Vol. 7, No. 1, January 1976, p. 31, cited in Kasun, *The War Against Population*, p. 85.
22. Chris Hedges, "U.S. Is Key Player in Controversial Birth Control Plan," *Christian Science Monitor*, January 13, 1984, p. 8, cited in Kasun, *The War Against Population*, p. 91.
23. Betsy Hartmann and Jane Hughes, "And the Poor Get Sterilized," *The Nation*, June 30, 1984, pp. 798-800, cited in Kasun, *The War Against Population*, p. 91.

24. The Population Council, *Studies in Family Planning*, Vol. 7, No. 1, January 1976, p. 31, cited in Kasun, *The War Against Population*, p. 85.

25. The Population Council, *Studies in Family Planning*, Vol. 4, No. 9, September 1973; The Population Council, "Thailand," *Country Profiles*, March 1972; World Bank, *Annual Reports: Statistical Abstract of the United States*, 1975, p. 319, cited in Kasun, *The War Against Population*, p. 87.

26. The Population Council, "Thailand," *Country Profiles,* pp. 10-11, cited in Kasun, *The War Against Population*, p. 88.

27. Greer, *Sex and Destiny*, pp. 352-353.

28. *Ibid.*, pp. 356-359.

29. *Ibid.*, p. 349.

30. Thomas M. Shapiro, *Population Control Politics: Women, Sterilization, and Reproductive Choice* (Philadelphia, Penn.: Temple University Press, 1985), p. 107.

31. *Policy Statement of the United States of America at the United Nations International Conference on Population (2nd session)*, Mexico, D.F., August 6-13, 1984, cited in Kasun, *The War Against Population*, pp. 92-93.

32. Kasun, *The War Against Population*, p. 94.

33. Gary North, *Is the World Running Down? Crisis in the Christian Worldview* (Tyler, Texas: Institute for Christian Economics, 1988), p. 146.

34. *Ibid.*, p. 147.

Chapter 10:
China's Self-inflicted
Genocide

1. Steven Mosher, "Forced Abortions and Infanticide in Communist China," *The Human Life Review*, Summer 1985, pp. 7-8.
2. *Ibid.*, p. 21.
3. *Ibid.*, p. 20.
4. Judith Banister, *China's Changing Population* (Stanford, Calif.: Stanford University Press, 1987), p. 195.
5. Mosher, "Forced Abortions and Infanticide in Communist China," pp. 7-8.
6. Banister, *China's Changing Population*, p. 191.
7. Mosher, "Forced Abortions and Infanticide in Communist China," p. 17.
8. Christopher Wren, "Chinese Region Showing Resistance to National Goals for Birth Control," *New York Times*, May 16, 1982, cited in Kasun, *The War Against Population*, p. 90.
9. Mosher, "Forced Abortions and Infanticide in Communist China," p. 23.
10. *Ibid.*, p. 28.
11. "Gender-selective Abortions," *Christianity Today*, April 17, 1987, p. 43.
12. Mosher, "Forced Abortions and Infanticide in Communist China," p. 28.
13. "Implications of Worldwide Population Growth for U.S. Security and Overseas Interests," p. 14, cited in Kasun, *The War Against Population*, pp. 79-80.

14. The World Bank, *World Development Report 1984*, pp. 123-124, 160; UN Fund for Population Activities, *1981 Report*, p. 52; Population Reference Bureau, *Intercom*, March/April 1983, p. 7; Lester Brown, *Worldwatch Paper* No. 53; International Planned Parenthood Federation, *People*, Vol. 10, No. 1, 1983, p. 24; cited in Kasun, *The War Against Population*, p. 92.

15. International Planned Parenthood Federation, *Report to Donors*, 1980, p. 40; UN Fund for Population Activities, *Reports* for 1980, 1981, 1982, 1983; cited in Kasun, p. 90.

Chapter 11:
Sweden:
America's Forerunner?

1. Coretta Scott King, "U.S. could learn much from Sweden," *The Tuscaloosa News*, April 12, 1988.

2. David Popenoe, "What Is Happening to the Family in Sweden?" *Social Change in Sweden*, December 1986, pp. 1-7; Neil Gilbert, "Sweden's Disturbing Family Trends," *The Wall Street Journal*, June 24, 1987; Sheila B. Kamerman, "Child Care Services: an Issue for Gender, Equity and Women's Solidarity," *Child Welfare*, 64, May/June 1985, p. 264; cited in Bryce Christensen, "Political Turmoil at America's 'Marriage Gap,'" *The Family in America*, April 1988, p. 6.

3. *Ibid.*

4. Allan C. Carlson, "The 'Population Question' Returns," *Persuasion at Work*, December 1985, p.5.

5. Allan C. Carlson, "Toward 'The Working Family': The Hidden Agenda Behind the Comparable Worth Debate," *Persuasion at Work*, July 1984, p. 3.

6. *Ibid.*, p. 4.

7. *Ibid.*, p. 5.

8. Allan C. Carlson, "Forward to the Past: Rebuilding Family Life in Post-Socialist Sweden," *The Family in America*, July 1992, p. 3.

9. Wattenberg, *The Birth Dearth*, p. 68.

10. Christensen, "Political Turmoil at America's 'Marriage Gap,'" p. 7.

11. Allan C. Carlson, "Suburb-Bashing and Other Feminine Acts," *Persuasion at Work*, May 1984, p. 7, cited in Bryce Christensen, "The Family as America's 'Captive Nation,'" *Persuasion at Work*, September 1986, p. 2.

12. Michael Levin, "Feminism, Stage Three," *Commentary*, August 1986, p. 29, cited in Bryce Christensen, "The Family as America's 'Captive Nation,'" p. 2.

13. Gary Bauer, chairman of the Family Research Council, cited in Christina F. Jeffrey, "Restoring the Balance: Finding a Way Out of the Social Security Crisis," *The Family in America*, February, 1992, p. 6.

14. Vance Packard, *Our Endangered Children: Growing Up in Our Changing World* (Boston: Little, Brown, 1983), p. 140, cited in Bryce Christensen, "The Family as America's 'Captive Nation,'" p. 3.

15. Christensen, "The Family as America's 'Captive Nation,'" p. 3.

16. George Dullea, "No-fault divorce hurts women and children most," *The Tuscaloosa News*, December 26, 1985, p. 6.
17. *Ibid.*
18. Packard, *Our Endangered Children*, pp. 185-202, cited in Christensen, "The Family as America's 'Captive Nation,'" p. 3.
19. Christensen, "The Family as America's 'Captive Nation,'" p. 3.
20. "The Growing Welfare State and the Shrinking Maternity Ward," *The Family in America New Research*, April 1987, p. 3.
21. Cheryl Russell, editor of *American Demographics* magazine, quoted in Michael Sivy, "Kids may be your best investment," *Money* Special Anniversary Issue, Fall 1987, p. 28.
22. Elizabeth Warnock Fernea, *Behind the Veil*, cited in Greer, *Sex and Destiny*, p. 24.

Chapter 12:
Prosperity and Posterity

1. Dorothy Field and Meredith Minkler, "Continuity and Change in Social Support Between Young-Old and Old-Old or Very-Old Age," *Journal of Gerontology* 43 [1988], pp. 100-106, cited in "The Best Is Yet to Be," *The Family in America New Research*, October 1988, p. 2.
2. Tim Stafford, "His Father's Son," *Christianity Today,* April 22, 1988, p. 21.